Aries

Aries

Sasha Fenton and Jonathan Dee

Aquarian
An Imprint of HarperCollinsPublishers

Aquarian
An Imprint of HarperCollins*Publishers*
77–85 Fulham Palace Road
Hammersmith, London W6 8JB
1160 Battery Street
San Francisco, California 94111–1213

First published by Aquarian 1994
10 9 8 7 6 5 4 3 2 1

A catalogue record for this book
is available from the British Library

ISBN 1 85538 393 4

Phototypeset by Harper Phototypesetters Limited,
Northampton, England
Printed in Great Britain by HarperCollinsManufacturing Glasgow

Contents

Aries in a Nutshell   1

Your Sun Sign   3

All the Other Sun Signs   5

You and Yours   16

The Elements and Qualities   28

The Pyramid of Passion   32

Aries in Love   35

Rising Signs   38

How the Rising Sign Modifies your Sun Sign   41

Aries in 1995   44

Aries in a Nutshell

YOUR RULING PLANET Your ruling body is the red planet, Mars. Once the Roman god of war, Mars has always been thought of as aggressive and dynamic.

YOUR SYMBOL The Ram is the symbol for your sign. This first appeared in ancient Egypt, representing the first of the gods, Ammon, which is very apt for the first sign of the zodiac. Aries was once also symbolized by the goose, although the origins of that have been lost in the mists of time.

PART OF THE BODY Aries rules the head, eyes, skull and upper jaw. Ariens are often red-haired when young. Many Aries men lose their hair in middle age. A mole, scar or other mark on the forehead is quite common. You should have a small nose and chin, and low cheek bones.

YOUR GOOD BITS Your best qualities are energy and initiative, a capacity for hard work and a love of life.

YOUR BAD BITS Your worst qualities are selfishness, impatience, aggression and a lack of thoroughness.

YOUR WEAKNESS Fast cars, fast lovers, fast food.

YOUR BEST DAY Tuesday. Aries is ruled by the god Mars and Tuesday is Mars's day.

YOUR WORST DAY In theory, Friday, but Ariens often love 'thank God it's Friday', because it means the weekend is on the way.

YOUR COLOUR Bright crimson red.

CITIES Birmingham, Blackburn, Florence, Naples, Boston, Sydney.

COUNTRIES England, Germany, Japan, Indonesia.

HOLIDAYS Anywhere where there is plenty to look at and lots of shops. The markets of Bangkok are the Arien's spiritual home.

LANDSCAPES Hilly, sandy ground, good for pasture, poor for crops. Anywhere that is not too hot but which has a history or ancient connections.

FOODS Most Ariens are unfussy eaters but traditional astrology suggests onions, radishes and garlic or anything else with a sharp flavour.

YOUR HERBS Basil, witch hazel.

YOUR TREES Thorn, chestnut.

YOUR FLOWERS Honeysuckle.

YOUR ANIMALS Vulture, fox, ostrich, leopard. Also the sheep or ram, of course.

YOUR METAL The metal associated with your sign is iron. Iron has a low melting point and was traditionally the metal from which weapons were made. Rusty iron is a reddish colour.

YOUR GEMS Aries has various gems associated with it, including the hard unyielding diamond and the passionate bloodstone.

MODE OF DRESS Anything new! You love buying clothes. Your taste may be plain or flamboyant but you love new things. You seek to disguise a large behind.

YOUR CAREERS Any large organization. Sports, medicine, engineering, teaching, or anything that involves wearing a uniform. Ariens make excellent mediums and writers too.

YOUR FRIENDS Honest, energetic, intelligent and generous people.

YOUR ENEMIES Devious or indecisive types or penny-pinching nit-pickers.

Your Sun Sign

Aries

Ruled by Mars
21st March to 20th April

Yours is a masculine, fire sign and your symbol is the ram. This combination gives you courage, a love of adventure and travel, energy, initiative and a determination to live life to the full.

Impulsive, enterprising, energetic, self-centred, generous, courageous, pioneering, highly-sexed . . . . Does this fit you? Well, some of it probably does but there are other rather different sides to your personality. For instance, you love your home and, whether it is a complete tip or a palace, it is yours and nobody is going to take it away from you. You like your family and you are probably quite happy in your marriage or partnership. Some Ariens get off on the wrong foot in partnerships, admit failure and bring the relationship to an end but, having done so, they go on to choose more wisely the second time around and really make a go of things. Some of you hang on to outworn relationships long after they have come to an end, probably due to possessive feelings about those things which you once owned. Some of you cling to your children long after they should have left the nest, others would love to see your kids off your hands but find it difficult to get them out of the house and out of your hair.

Ariens of both sexes can fall madly in love and then drive yourselves, not to mention your friends, completely crazy while you extol the virtues of your beloved or wonder aloud for the umpteenth time, 'Just where is this relationship going?' Although you love the early and exciting stages of a courtship, you are happier and more relaxed when in something more comfortable and enduring. Sex is an important part of any relationship for you and you will not stay with a partner for long if this is denied you. Some Ariens are happy to have plenty of straightforward lovemaking, while others can be real fantasy merchants who want to dress up as King Charles or Nell Gwyn – or whatever else captures your imagination.

You are competitive as well as somewhat impulsive but you don't take chances where it matters. For example, you may slog onwards with a fairly uninspiring job, whilst pitting all your energy and competitiveness against others in a sporting activity or a hobby of some kind. You are happy to work in a large organization, perhaps in a leadership position, and many of you seem to land up in jobs which require specialized clothing or hard hats.

You are extremely sociable, fond of a meal out and also a drink or two to go with it. At any kind of function, you can be seen hopping and bopping and flirting like mad with anyone who catches your eye. You can't take too much sitting around indoors and you need something to look forward to at weekends. You are happy to spend money on entertainments but you can be surprisingly stingy about other things.

One really typical Aries peculiarity is your behaviour towards visitors. You sit them down with a drink, biscuit and anything else they may need, you make sure that they are comfortable enough and then, just when they begin to settle down for a good old gossip, you walk out of the room, leaving them sitting there!

All the Other Sun Signs

Taurus

These people are practical and persevering. Taureans are solid and reliable, regular in habits, sometimes a bit wet behind the ears and stubborn as mules. Their love of money and the comfort which it can bring may make them very materialistic in outlook. They are most suited to a practical career which brings with it few surprises and plenty of money. However, they have a strong artistic streak which can be expressed in work, hobbies and interests.

Some Taureans are quick and clever, highly amusing and quite outrageous in appearance, but underneath this crazy exterior is a background of true talent and very hard work. This type may be a touch arrogant. Other Taureans hate to be rushed or hassled, preferring to work quietly and thoroughly at their own pace. These people take relationships very seriously and they make safe and reliable partners. They may keep their worries to themselves but they are not usually liars or sexually untrustworthy.

Being so very sensual as well as patient, these people make excellent lovers. Their biggest downfall comes later in life when they have a tendency to plonk themselves down in front of the television night after night, tuning out the rest of the world. Another problem with some Taureans is their 'pet hate'. This is something which has long since got under their skins and which they go on about at any given opportunity. Their virtues are common sense, loyalty, responsibility and a pleasant, non-hostile approach to others. Taureans are much brighter than anyone gives them credit for and it is hard to beat them in an argument because they usually know what they are talking about. If a Taurean is on your side, they make wonderful friends and comfortable and capable colleagues.

Gemini

Geminis are often accused of being short on intellect and unable to stick to anyone or anything for long. In short, great fun at a party but totally unreliable. This is unfair: nobody works harder, is more reliable or capable than a Gemini when he or she puts their mind to a task, especially if there is a chance of making large sums of money! Unfortunately, Geminis have a low boredom threshold and they can drift away from something or someone when it no longer interests them. They like to be busy, with plenty of variety in their lives and the opportunity to communicate with others. Their forte is the communications industry where they shamelessly pinch ideas and improve on them. Many Geminis are highly ambitious people who won't allow anything or anyone to stand in their way.

They are surprisingly constant in relationships, often marrying for life but, if things don't work out, they will walk out and put the experience behind them. Geminis need relationships and if one fails, they will soon start looking for the next. Faithfulness is another story, because the famed Gemini curiosity can lead to any number of adventures. Geminis educate their children well while neglecting to see whether they have a clean shirt to put on.

The house is full of books, videos, televisions, CDs, newspapers and magazines and there is a phone in every room as well as in the car, the loo and in a Gemini lady's handbag.

Cancer

Cancerians look for security on the one hand and adventure and novelty on the other. They are popular because they really listen to what others are saying. Their own voices are attractive too. They are naturals for sales work and in any kind of advisory capacity. Where their own problems are concerned, they can disappear inside themselves and brood, which makes them hard for others to understand. Cancerians spend a good deal of time worrying about their families and, even more so, about money. They appear soft but are very hard to influence.

Many Cancerians are small traders and many more work in teaching or the caring professions. They have a feel for history, perhaps collecting historical mementos, and their memory is excellent. They need to have a home but they love to travel away from it, being happy in the knowledge that it is there waiting for them to come back to. There are some Cancerians who seem to drift through life and expect other members of their family to keep them.

Romantically, they prefer to be settled and they fear being alone. A marriage would need to be really bad before they left, and if they do, they soon look for a new partner. These people can be scoundrels in business because they hate parting with money once they have their hands on it. However, their charm and intelligence usually manage to keep them out of trouble.

Leo

Leos can be marvellous company or a complete pain in the neck. Under normal circumstances, they are warmhearted, generous, sociable and popular but they can be very moody and irritable when under pressure or under the weather. Leos put their heart and soul into whatever they are doing and they can work like demons for a while; but they cannot keep up the pace for long, soon needing to get away, zonk out on the sofa or take one of their frequent holidays. These people always appear confident and they look like true winners, but their confidence can suddenly evaporate, leaving them unsure and unhappy with their efforts. They are extremely sensitive to hurt and they cannot take ridicule or even very much teasing.

Leos are proud, they have very high standards in all that they do and most of them have great integrity and honesty, but there are some who are complete and utter crooks. These people can stand on their dignity and be very snobbish. Their arrogance can become insufferable and they can take their powers of leadership into the realms of bossiness. They are convinced that they should be in charge and they can be very obstinate. They love the status and lifestyle which proclaims their successes. Many Leos work in glamour professions such as an airline or the entertainment industry. Others spend their day communing with computers and other high-tech gadgetry. In loving relationships, they are loyal but only while the magic lasts. If boredom sets in, they can start looking around for fresh fields. They are the most generous and loving of people and they love affection. Leos are kind, charming and they live life to the full.

Virgo

Virgos are highly intelligent, interested in everything and everyone and happy to be busy with many jobs and hobbies. Many have some kind of specialized knowledge and most are good with their hands. Their nit-picking ways can infuriate their colleagues. They find it hard to discuss their innermost feelings and this can make them hard to understand. In many ways, they are happier doing something practical than dealing with relationships. These people can overdo the self-sacrificial bit and make themselves martyrs to other people's impractical lifestyles. They are willing to fit in with whatever is going on and they can adjust to any kind of lifestyle but mustn't neglect their own needs.

Although excellent communicators and wonderfully witty conversationalists, Virgos prefer to express their deepest feelings by actions rather than words. Most Virgos avoid touching all but very close friends and family members and they find lovey-dovey behaviour embarrassing. These people can be very highly sexed and they may use this as a way of expressing love. Virgoans are criticized a good deal as children and often made to feel unwelcome in their childhood homes. They in turn become very critical of others and they can use this in order to wound.

Many Virgos overcome inhibitions by taking up acting, music, cookery or sports. Acting is particularly common to this sign because it allows them to put aside their fears and take on the mantle of someone quite different. They are shy and slow to make friends but when they do accept someone, they are the most loyal, gentle and kind of companions. They are excellent company with the greatest sense of humour.

Libra

Librans have a deceptive appearance, looking soft but being tough and quite selfish underneath. Astrological tradition tells us that this sign is dedicated to marriage, but a high proportion of Librans prefer to remain single, particularly when a difficult relationship comes to an end. These people are great to tell secrets to because they never listen to anything properly and promptly forget whatever was said. The confusion between their desire to co-operate with others and the need for self-expression is even more evident when at work. The best job is one where they are a part of an organization but are able to make their own decisions.

While some Librans are shy and lacking in confidence, others are strong and determined with definite leadership qualities. All need to find a job which entails dealing with others and which does not wear out their delicate nerves. All Librans are charming, sophisticated, diplomatic and confusing to others. All have a strong sense of justice and fair play but most haven't the strength to take on a determinedly lame duck. They project an image which is attractive, chosen to represent their sense of status and refinement. Being inclined to experiment sexually, they are not the most faithful of partners and even goody goody Librans are terrible flirts.

Scorpio

Reliable, resourceful and enduring, Scorpios seem to be the strong men and women of the zodiac. But are they really? They can be nasty at times, dishing out what they see as the truth, no matter how unwelcome. Their own feelings are sensitive and they are easily hurt, but they won't allow others to see their vulnerable side. When they are very low or unhappy, they get ill. However, they have great resilience and they bounce back time and again from the most awful ailments.

Nobody needs to love and be loved more than a Scorpio, but their partners must stand up to them because they will give anyone they don't respect a very hard time indeed. They are the most loyal and honest of companions, both in personal relationships and at work. One reason for this is their hatred of change or uncertainty. Scorpios enjoy being the power behind the throne with someone else occupying the hot seat. This way, they can quietly manipulate everyone, set one against another and get exactly what they want from the situation.

Scorpios' voices are their best feature, often low, well-modulated and cultured and these wonderful voices are used to the full in pleasant persuasion. These people are neither as highly sexed nor as difficult to get along with as most astrology books make out, but they do have their passions (even if these are not always for sex itself) and they like to be thought of as sexy. They love to shock and to appear slightly dangerous but they also make kind-hearted and loyal friends, great hosts and gentle people who are often very fond of animals.

Sagittarius

Sagittarians are great company because they are interested in everything and everyone. Broad-minded and lacking in prejudice, they are fascinated by even the strangest of people. With their optimism and humour, they are often the life and soul of the party, while they are in a good mood; they can become down-hearted, crabby and awkward on occasion but not usually for long. Sagittarians can be hurtful to others because they cannot resist speaking what they see as the truth, even if it causes embarrassment. However, their tactlessness is usually innocent and they have no desire to hurt.

Sagittarians need an unconventional lifestyle, preferably one which allows them to travel. They cannot be cooped up in a cramped environment and they need to meet new people and to explore a variety of ideas during their day's work. Money is not their god, they will work for a pittance if they feel inspired by the task. Their values are spiritual rather than material. Many are attracted to the spiritual side of life and may be interested in the Church, philosophy, astrology and other new age subjects. Higher education and legal matters attract them because these subjects expand and explore intellectual boundaries. Long-lived relationships may not appeal because they need to feel free and unfettered, but they can do well with a self-sufficient and independent partner. Despite all this intellectualism and need for freedom, Sagittarians have a deep need to be cuddled and touched and they need to be supported emotionally.

Capricorn

Capricorns are patient, realistic and responsible and they take life seriously. They need security but they may find this difficult to achieve. Many live on a treadmill of work, simply to pay the bills and they take their family responsibilities seriously, even caring for distant relatives if this becomes necessary. However, they can play the martyr while doing so. These people hate coarseness, they are easily embarrassed and they hate to annoy anyone. They believe fervently in keeping the peace in their families. This doesn't mean that they cannot stand up for themselves, indeed they know how to get their own way and they won't be bullied.

They are adept at using charm to get around prickly people.

Capricorns are ambitious and hard working, patient and status-conscious and they will work their way steadily towards the top in any organization. If they run their own business, they need a partner with more pizzazz than they have to deal with sales and marketing, while they keep an eye on the books. Their nit-picking habits can infuriate others and some have a tendency to 'know best' and not to listen. These people work at their hobbies with the same kind of dedication that they put into everything else. They are faithful and reliable in relationships and it takes a great deal to make them stray. If a relationship breaks up, they take a long time to get over it. They either marry very early or delay serious relationships until middle age when they are less shy. As an earth sign, Capricorns are highly sexed but they need to be in a relationship where they can relax and gain confidence. Their best attribute is their genuine kindness and their wonderfully dry, witty sense of humour.

Aquarius

Clever, friendly, kind and humane, Aquarians are the easiest people to make friends with but probably the hardest really to know. They are often more comfortable with friends and acquaintances than with those who are close to them. Being dutiful, they would never let a member of their family go without their basic requirements, but they can be strangely, even deliberately, blind to their loved ones' underlying needs and real feelings. They are more comfortable with causes and their idealistic ideas than with the day-to-day routine of family life. Their homes may reflect this lack of interest by being rather messy, although there are other Aquarians who are almost clinically house proud.

Their opinions are formed early in life and are firmly fixed. Being patient with people, they make good teachers and are, themselves, always willing to learn something new. But are they willing to go out and earn a living? Some are, many are not. These people can be extremely eccentric in the way they dress or the way they live. They make a point of being 'different' and they can actually feel very unsettled and uneasy if made to conform, even outwardly. Their restless, sceptical minds mean that they need an alternative kind of lifestyle which stretches them mentally.

In relationships, they are surprisingly constant and faithful and they only stray when they know in their hearts that there is no longer anything to be gained from staying put. Aquarians are often very attached to the first real commitment in their lives and they can even re-marry a previously divorced partner. Their sexuality fluctuates, perhaps high for some years then pushed aside while something else occupies their energies, then high again. Many Aquarians are extremely highly sexed and very clever and active in bed.

Pisces

This idealistic, dreamy, kind and impractical sign needs a lot of understanding. They have a fractured personality which has so many sides and so many moods that they probably don't even understand themselves. Nobody is kinder, more thoughtful and caring, but they have a tendency to drift away from people and responsibilities. When the going gets rough, they go! Being creative, clever and resourceful, these people can achieve a great deal and really reach the top, but few of them do. Some Pisceans have a self-destruct button which they press before reaching their goal. Others do achieve success and the motivating force behind this essentially spiritual and mystical sign is often *money*. Many Pisceans feel insecure, most suffer some experience of poverty in their early lives and they grow into adulthood determined that they will never feel that kind of uncertainty again.

Pisceans are at home in any kind of creative or caring career. Many can be found in teaching, nursing and the arts. Some find life hard and are often unhappy; many have to make tremendous sacrifices on behalf of others. This may be a pattern which repeats itself from childhood, where the message is that the Piscean's needs always come last. These people can be stubborn, awkward, selfish and quite nasty when a friendship or relationship goes sour. This is because, despite their basically kind and gentle personality, there is a side which needs to be in charge of any relationship. Pisceans make extremely faithful partners as long as the romance doesn't evaporate and as long as their partners treat them well. Problems occur if they are mistreated or rejected, if they become bored or restless, or if their alcohol intake climbs over the danger level. These people are sexual fantasists so, in this sphere of life, anything can happen!

You and Yours

What is it like to bring up a Taurean child? What kind of father does an Aquarian make? How does it feel to grow up with a Scorpio mother? Whatever your own sign is, how do you appear to your parents and how do you behave towards your children?

The Aries Father

Arien men take the duties of fatherhood very seriously. They read to their children, take them on educational trips and expose them to art and music from an early age. They can push their children too hard or tyrannize the sensitive ones. The Aries father wants his children not only to *have* what he didn't have but also to *be* what he isn't. He respects those children who are high achievers and who can stand up to him.

The Aries Mother

Arien women love their children dearly and will make amazing sacrifices for them – but don't expect them to give up their jobs or their outside interests for motherhood. Competitive herself, this mother wants her children to be the best and she may push them too hard. However, she is kind hearted, affectionate and not likely to over-discipline them. She treats her offspring as adults and is well loved in return.

The Aries Child

Arien children are hard to ignore. Lively, noisy and demanding, they try to enjoy every moment of their childhood. Despite this, they lack confidence and need reassurance. Often clever but lacking in self-discipline, they need to be made to attend school each day and to do their homework. Active and competitive, these children excel in sports, dancing or learning to play a pop music instrument.

The Taurus Father

This man cares deeply for his children and wants the best for them but he doesn't expect the impossible. He may lay the law down and he can be unsympathetic to the attitudes and interests of a new generation. He may frighten young children by shouting at them. Being a responsible parent, he offers a secure family base but he may find it hard to let them go when they want to leave.

The Taurus Mother

These women make good mothers due to their highly domesticated nature. Some are real earth mothers, baking bread and making wonderful toys and games for their children. Sane and sensible but not highly imaginative, they do best with a child who has ordinary needs and they get confused by those who are 'special' in any way. Taurus mothers are very loving but they use reasonable discipline when necessary.

The Taurus Child

Taurean children can be surprisingly demanding. Their loud voices and stubborn natures can be irritating. Plump, sturdy and strong, some are shy and retiring, while others can bully weaker children. Artistic, sensual, often musical; these children can lose themselves in creative or beautiful hobbies. They need to be encouraged to share and to express love and also to avoid too many sweet foods.

The Gemini Father

Geminian fathers are fairly laid back in their approach and, while they cope well with fatherhood, they can become bored with home life and try to escape from their duties. Some are so absorbed with work that they hardly see their offspring. At home, Gemini fathers will provide books, educational toys and as much computer equipment as the child can use and they enjoy a family game of tennis.

The Gemini Mother

These mothers can be very pushy because they see education as the road to success. She encourages a child to pursue any interest and will sacrifice time and money for this. They usually have a job outside the home and may rely on other people to do some child minding for them. Their children cannot always count on coming home to a balanced meal, but they can talk to their mothers on any subject.

The Gemini Child

These children needs a lot of reassurance because they often feel like square pegs in round holes. They either do very well at school incurring the wrath of less able children, or they fail dismally and have to make it up later in life. They learn to read early and some have excellent mechanical ability, while others excel at sports. They get bored very easily and can be extremely irritating.

The Cancer Father

A true family man who will happily to embrace even step-children as if they were his own. Letting go of the family when they grow up is another matter. Cancerian sulks, moodiness and bouts of childishness can confuse or frighten some children while his changeable attitude to money can make them unsure of what they should ask for. This father enjoys home making and child rearing and he may be happy to swap roles.

The Cancer Mother

Cancerian women are excellent homemakers and cheerful and reasonable mothers as long as they have a part-time job or an interest outside the house. They instinctively know when a child is unhappy and can deal with it in a manner which is both efficient and loving. These women have a reputation for clinging but most are quite realistic when the time comes for their brood to leave the nest.

The Cancer Child

These children are shy, cautious and slow to grow up. They may achieve little at school, 'disappearing' behind louder and more demanding classmates. They can be worriers who complain about every ache and pain or suffer from imaginary fears. They may take on the mother's role in the family, dictating to their sisters and brothers at times. Gentle and loving but moody and secretive, they need a lot of love and encouragement.

The Leo Father

These men can be wonderful fathers as long as they remember that children are not simply small and rather obstreperous adults. Leo fathers like to be involved with their children and encourage them to do well at school. They happily make sacrifices for their children and they truly want them to have the best, but they can be a bit too strict and they may demand too high a standard.

The Leo Mother

Leo mothers are very caring and responsible. Although they cannot be satisfied with a life of pure domesticity, they can combine motherhood with a job. These mothers don't fuss about minor details and are prepared to put up with a certain amount of noise and disruption but they can be irritable and they may demand too much of their children.

The Leo Child

These children know almost from the day they are born that they are special; they are usually loved and wanted but they are also aware that a lot is expected from them. Leo children appear outgoing but they are surprisingly sensitive and easily hurt. They only seem to wake up to the need to study a day or so after they leave school, but they find a way to make a success of their lives.

The Virgo Father

These men may be embarrassed by open declarations of love and affection and find it hard to give cuddles and reassurance to small children. Yet they love their offspring dearly and will go to any lengths to see that they have the best possible education and outside activities. Virgoan men can become wrapped up in their work, forgetting to spend time relaxing and playing with their children.

The Virgo Mother

Virgoan women try hard to be good mothers because they probably had a poor childhood themselves. They love their children very much and want the best for them but they may be fussy about unnecessary details such as dirt on the kitchen floor or the state of the children's school books. If they can keep their tensions and longings away from their children, they can be the most kindly and loving parents.

The Virgo Child

Virgoan children are practical and capable and may do very well at school, but they are not always happy. They don't always fit in and they find it difficult to make friends. They may be shy, modest and sensitive and they can find it hard to reach their own impossibly high standards. Virgo children don't need harsh discipline, they want approval and will usually respond perfectly well to reasoned argument.

The Libra Father

Libran men mean well, but they may not actually perform that well. They have no great desire to be fathers but welcome their children when they come along. They may slide out of the more irksome tasks by having an absorbing job or a series of equally absorbing hobbies which keep them occupied outside the home. These men do better with older children because they can talk to them.

The Libra Mother

Libran mothers are pleasant and easy going but some of them are more interested in their looks, their furnishings and their friends than their children. Others are very loving and kind but a bit too soft, which results in their children disrespecting them or walking all over them later in life. These mothers enjoy talking to their children and encouraging them to succeed.

The Libra Child

These children are charming and attractive and they have no difficulty in getting on with people. They make just enough effort to get through school and to do such household jobs as they cannot dodge. They may drive their parents mad with their demands for the latest gadget or gimmick. However, their common sense, sense of humour and reasonable attitude makes harsh discipline unnecessary.

The Scorpio Father

These fathers can be really awful or absolutely wonderful; there are no half measures. Good Scorpio men provide love and security because they stick closely to their homes and families and are unlikely to do a disappearing act. Difficult ones can be loud and tyrannical. These proud men want their children to be the best.

The Scorpio Mother

These mothers are either wonderful or not really maternal at all, although they try to do their best. If they take to child rearing, they encourage their offspring educationally and in their hobbies. These mothers have no time for whiny or miserable children but they respect outgoing, talented and courageous ones.

The Scorpio Child

Scorpio children are competitive, self-centred and unwilling to co-operate with brothers, sisters, teachers or anyone else when in an awkward mood. They can be deeply unreadable, living in a world of their own and filled with all kinds of strange angry feelings. At other times, they can be delightfully caring companions. They love animals, sports, children's organizations and group activities.

The Sagittarius Father

Sagittarian fathers will give their children all the education they can stand. They happily provide books, equipment and take their offspring out to see anything interesting. They may not always be available to their offspring, but they make up for it by surprising their family with tickets for sporting events or by bringing home a baby rabbit. These men are cheerful and childlike themselves.

The Sagittarius Mother

This mother is kind, easy going and pleasant. She may be very ordinary with suburban standards or she may be unbelievably eccentric, forcing the family to take up strange diets and filling the house with weird and wonderful people. Some opt out of child rearing by finding child minders while others take on other people's children and a host of animals in addition to their own.

The Sagittarius Child

Sagittarian children love animals and the outdoor life but they are also as interested in sitting around and watching the telly as the next child. These children have plenty of friends whom they rush out and visit at every opportunity. Happy and optimistic but highly independent, they cannot be pushed in any direction. Many leave home in late teens in order to travel.

The Capricorn Father

These are true family men who cope with housework and child rearing but they are sometimes too involved in work to spend much time at home. Dutiful and caring, these men are unlikely to run off with a bimbo or to leave their family wanting. However, they can be stuffy or out of touch with the younger generation. They encourage their children to do well and to behave properly.

The Capricorn Mother

Capricornian women make good mothers but they may be inclined to fuss. Being ambitious, they want their children to do well and they teach them to respect teachers, youth leaders and so on. These mothers usually find work outside the home in order to supplement the family income. They are very loving but they can be too keen on discipline and the careful management of pocket money.

The Capricorn Child

Capricorn children are little adults from the day they are born. They don't need much discipline or encouragement to do well at school. Modest and well behaved, they are almost too good to be true. However, they suffer badly with their nerves and can suffer from ailments such as asthma. They need to be taught to let go, have fun and enjoy their childhood. Some are too selfish or ambitious to make friends.

The Aquarian Father

Some Aquarian men have no great desire to be fathers but they make a reasonable job of it when they have to. They cope best when their children are reasonable and intelligent but, if they are not, they tune out and ignore them. Some Aquarians will spend hours inventing games and toys for their children while all of them value education and try to push their children.

The Aquarian Mother

Some of these mothers are too busy putting the world to rights to see what is going on in their own family. However, they are kind, reasonable and keen on education. They may be busy outside the house but they often take their children along with them. Not being fussy homemakers they are happy to have all the neighbourhood kids in the house. They respect a child's dignity.

The Aquarian Child

Aquarian children may be demanding when very young but they become much more reasonable when at school. They are easily bored and need outside interests. They have many friends and may spend more time in other people's homes than in their own. Very stubborn and determined, they make it quite clear from an early age that they intend to do things their own way. These children suffer from nerves.

The Pisces Father

Piscean men fall into one of two categories. Some are kind and gentle, happy to be take their children on outings and to introduce them to art, culture, music or sport. Others are disorganized and unpredictable. The kindly fathers don't always push their children. They encourage their kids to have friends and a pet or two.

The Pisces Mother

Piscean mothers may be lax and absent minded but they love their children and are usually loved in return. Many are too disorganized to run a perfect household so meals, laundry etc. can be hit and miss; their children prosper despite this, although many learn to reverse the mother/child roles. These mothers teach their offspring to appreciate animals and the environment.

The Pisces Child

These sensitive children may find life difficult and they can get lost among stronger, more demanding brothers and sisters. They may drive their parents batty with their dreamy attitude and they can make a fuss over nothing. They need a secure and loving home with parents who shield them from harsh reality while encouraging them to develop their imaginative and psychic abilities.

The Elements and Qualities

The Elements

You will notice throughout this book that we use such terms as earth, air, fire and water to describe the characteristics of the signs. We also use the astrological terms of cardinal, fixed and mutable and we may occasionally mention that a sign is masculine and positive, or feminine and negative in nature. These terms are in common use in popular newspaper astrology nowadays, so you may as well know what they mean.

The Element of Fire
Fire signs are *Aries, Leo and Sagittarius*. These signs represent enthusiasm, initiative, intuition, optimism and faith in the future. Fire sign people never quite relinquish their childhood and are in tune with young people and young ideas. These entertaining people are egotistical and arrogant at times but they get things started. They create action and pace but they leave the details to others. Fire people are on the ball and they treat life like a game. They find it impossible to save money but they often earn their way out of disaster.

The Element of Earth
The earth signs are *Taurus, Virgo and Capricorn*. These signs represent security, structure, slow growth and concrete

results. Earth sign people are sensible, reliable and practical in outlook. They do things thoroughly, they can be fussy about details and they try to finish all that they start. They are unlikely to be extravagant and they may hold on to their money and possessions very tightly. They are very caring towards their family and close friends and they are mature, but they may lack spontaneity.

The Element of Air

The air signs are *Gemini, Libra and Aquarius*. Air signs are concerned with communication, networks of all kinds, education, theoretical ideas and finding answers to questions. Air sign people are keen on conversation and the picking up and passing on of ideas. They may be deeply academic or chirpy, streetwise types, but they are usually very up-to-date whatever their actual age.

The Element of Water

The water signs are *Cancer, Scorpio and Pisces*. Water signs are concerned with the emotions and feelings, the beginnings, endings and major transformations of life and also the moods and inner urges. Watery people respond slowly when asked a question and they take time over grasping new concepts. They are slow to change, preferring tried and tested paths. Their chief need is security. Faithful, loyal and often quite tense, these people have an intuitive feeling for what is right for themselves and their families. They are usually sensible and reliable but they can become depressed and ill when life doesn't go their way. Watery people are often artistic or musical.

The Qualities

Cardinal Signs

The cardinal signs are *Aries, Cancer, Libra and Capricorn*.

All these signs are ambitious either for themselves, their families, their organizations or all three. They like to feel that they are founding a dynasty and starting something which will still be there when they have gone.

Fixed Signs

The fixed signs are *Taurus, Leo, Scorpio and Aquarius*. All these signs are stubborn and determined and they don't change or adapt to new circumstances very easily. They stick to their jobs, their homes and their families as long as they can. They have the strength and determination to see things through and they work hard to have and to hold.

Mutable Signs

The mutable signs are *Gemini, Virgo, Sagittarius and Pisces*. These people have the courage to take their own very independent path and try new things. They are the bungee jumpers of the zodiac, launching themselves over the edge with a kind of crazy faith in their guardian spirits. Mutable people are adaptable and they will fit in with most situations. They try to find some point of understanding between themselves and the oddest of people. Their thinking is wider than the other two types and their friendliness and good humour allows them to see the funny side of even the nastiest situation. They are easily bored and may be addicted to travel, new faces, change for change's sake or simply being different. They often spend their early years feeling alone or lonely.

Masculine/Positive, Feminine/Negative

These signs alternate, with Aries, Gemini, Leo, Libra, Sagittarius and Aquarius being masculine/positive and Taurus, Cancer, Virgo, Scorpio, Capricorn and Pisces being feminine/negative.

The masculine/positive signs are *supposedly* outgoing,

sociable, decisive, confident, assertive and courageous.

The feminine/negative signs are *supposedly* introspective, shy, moody, receptive, unassertive, weak and fearful.

We say *supposedly* here because this theory doesn't entirely fit the facts.

The Pyramid of Passion

This section is designed to amuse. In reality, all the signs of the zodiac can find happiness with any one of the others – but you can have some fun finding out how *your* relationship fits into the Pyramid of Passion!

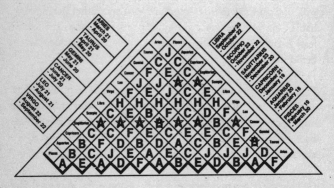

A This one should be fun. It's a strong match, compatible in every way. Well, at least you both want the same things. You are both in agreement and are washed in a sea of sentiment. No surprises in this one: it should last, if you don't get too bored.

B Very good. You fancy each other like mad and there should be plenty that would keep you laughing, and that's a good sign. The trouble is that one or other of you is a bit flighty, so don't expect the roving eye (and other parts of the body) to stop roving. Frivolous, but maybe too fickle to last!

C Not too bad as long as you are a tolerant sort of person. There'll be lots of different opinions and ideas, so it certainly won't get boring. In fact, your quarrels should put Burton and Taylor to shame, although the bedroom scene looks more promising.

D Possessive, passionate, powerful and intense. This one has all the ingredients of obsessive ardour. You'll be suspicious of everyone from the owner of the chippie down the road, to your own family. It could last, as long as you remember that not everybody wants to jump into bed with your other half.

E This should be a wild and wacky partnership. Initial attraction will soon give way to utter irritation with your other half's funny habits. On balance, your relationship will be best as friends: at least friends do eventually go home. As lovers, it's a case of tears before bedtime.

F Warning, this volcanic relationship warrants a public safety announcement! We're not saying that it won't work, but you are outmanned and generally run down. The doormat might bite back now and again, but most just get trodden on. Think again about who's calling the shots.

G This could be a magnetic attraction of opposites. Very sexy! The emotions stirred up are bound to dig very deep indeed. It's love or hate with nothing in between, and sometimes both at the same time. Never boring, the only problem is that sometimes you'll be speaking in a different language from each other.

H Forget it! As a lasting partnership, this is a no-no. You could write what you have in common on the back of a postage stamp.

So you may as well use the stamp on a postcard to someone who is more compatible. You enjoy sport, your lover enjoys the ballet, you want caviar, your lover wants chips. Call the whole thing off.

J Don't even think about it! If the two of you were stranded on a desert island together, you might just mate for the sake of something to do: that is, if you hadn't killed each other first. You have totally different ways of looking at life and utterly different needs. You can be friends of a sort, but never lovers. Be polite to each other – and keep your distance.

☆ The stars signify sizzling sensuality!

Aries in Love

You Need:

CHEERFULNESS Ariens of both sexes need a cheerful and chatty partner because you don't enjoy sitting around in silence. Your partner must be sociable and happy to make friends with your friends.

PASSION Yours is a strongly sexed sign and you need a lover who is as enthusiastic as you are. You need passion in a more general way, too, in that your partner should have interests or a job that he or she is passionate about. You hate people who are only half alive.

REASON You can't stand sulky or moody people, so your best bet is one who can let a certain amount roll off like water from a duck's back and who doesn't get into a strop over little things. Real anger for a real reason is something you can understand, especially if your partner is willing to do something about the problem.

You Give:

SUPPORT Whether your lover is housebound or bound up with a career, you try to help where you can. You will happily take on children, parents and other relatives as well as fixing the car or finding extra money. Both sexes hate housework and do it because you have to.

SEXUALITY You express your deepest feelings in a loving relationship and can end any argument by making love. You may lack sexual confidence when young but this improves when you are in a good relationship.

HUMOUR AND WIT You could be very clever and you are definitely very amusing. You have a fund of jokes and funny stories and you are good at telling them. You may be a good singer or dancer too. You are entertaining to live with.

What You Can Expect From the Other Zodiac Signs:

TAURUS *Security, stability, comfort.* The Taurean will stand by you and they will try to improve your financial position. They will create a beautiful home and garden for you.

GEMINI *Stimulation, encouragement, variety.* This lover will never bore you, they will always encourage you and they are always ready for an outing. They give emotional support too.

CANCER *Emotional security, companionship, help.* Cancerians will never leave you stranded at a party or alone when suffering from the flu. They always lend a hand when asked.

LEO *Affection, fun, loyalty.* Leo lovers are very steadfast and they would murder anyone who hurt one of their family. They enjoy romping and playing affectionate love games.

VIRGO *Clear thinking, kindness, humour.* Virgoans make intelligent and amusing partners. They can be critical but never unkind. They take responsibility towards you seriously.

LIBRA *Fair play, sensuality, advice.* Librans will listen to your problems and give balanced and sensible advice. They are wonderfully inventive and affectionate lovers too.

SCORPIO *Truth, passion, loyalty.* Scorpios will take your interests as seriously as they do their own. They will stick by you when the going gets rough and they won't flannel you.

SAGITTARIUS *Honesty, fun, novelty.* These lovers will never bore you and they will keep up whatever pace you set. They seek the truth and they don't keep their feelings hidden.

CAPRICORN *Companionship, common sense, laughter.* Capricorns enjoy doing things together and they won't leave you in the lurch when the going gets tough. They can make you laugh too.

AQUARIUS *Stimulation, friendship, sexuality.* Aquarians are friends as well as lovers. They are great fun because you never know what they are going to do next, in or out of bed.

PISCES *Sympathy, support, love.* These romantic lovers never let you down. They can take you with them into their personal fantasy world and they are always ready for a laugh.

Rising Signs

What is a Rising Sign?

Your rising sign is the sign of the zodiac which was climbing up over the eastern horizon at the moment when you were born. *This is not the same as your Sun sign.* The world turns completely round during the course of each day and all twelve zodiac signs appear to pass over the horizon during each twenty-four hour day, so you can see how important the right time of birth is in fixing the right rising sign. If you only have a vague idea of your time of birth, you will still be able to work out your rising sign by trial and error. If you want to look more closely at this aspect of astrology, try Sasha's book *Rising Signs*.

Can the Rising Sign Tell You More About Your Future?

The rising sign is as important as the Sun sign when it comes to tracking events so, if you want more help with your daily horoscopes, get a pal to buy you the book which corresponds to your rising sign as well as the one for your Sun sign!

Starting the Hunt For Your Rising Sign

Before you try your hand at the rising sign finder chart, you will have to work out whether you were born during Daylight Saving or during British Summer Time (when the clocks were forward): you may have to deduct one hour to bring your time of birth back to Greenwich Mean Time.

Please bear in mind that the method used in this book is very rough and ready. It will work with reasonable accuracy wherever you were born, although it would definitely be worth reading through the signs which precede and follow the one you pinpoint on the chart, just in case. If you want a really accurate birth chart with a dead accurate rising sign, then contact any postal astrology service or consultant astrologer in your area.

How to Use the Chart

1. On the top line, mark the time of your birth (deducting one hour if born during Daylight Saving or British Summer Time).
2. On the bottom line, mark the day and month of your birth.
3. Join the marks with a straight line. The point where this crosses denotes your rising sign.

Examples

Here are a couple of examples which we have worked out for you in order to demonstrate the system.

1. Jane Brown. Born in Brighton on 21st September at 7 a.m.

2. John Smith. Born in New York on 3rd May at 9 p.m.

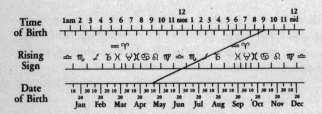

As you can see from the examples, Jane Brown's rising sign is Libra and John Smith's is Sagittarius.

What Does Your Rising Sign Tell You?

Many people seem, on the outside, more like their rising sun than their sun sign. Therefore, if you are habitually taken for a Taurean when you are, in fact, a Sagittarian, this could well be the reason. The rising sign may influence the kind of job you do and the way you behave out in the world. Most importantly, it may reflect the kind of programming and influence you received as a child.

You would find it very interesting, once you have worked out your own rising sign, to read the passage that matches it in the chapter entitled 'All the Other Sun Signs'. So, for example, if you find that you have Leo rising, read the Leo section on page 8 because it will tell you more about yourself.

How the Rising Sign Modifies your Sun Sign

The following chapter shows how your Sun sign might be modified by your rising sign. Read the rising sign which you think is yours and take a look at the one which precedes it and also the following one, just to check.

Aries with Aries Rising

This is Aries in its purest form and all the Arien traits are strongly marked. If you were born before dawn, you would be very outgoing and adventurous but, if you were born after the Sun had risen, you would be much quieter, artistic and drawn to mystical or psychic matters.

Aries with Taurus Rising

Your outer manner is fairly quiet and shy and you may be a keen musician, cook or gardener. You are more settled and less adventurous than other Ariens.

Aries with Gemini Rising

You are clever and quick thinking and you can do a dozen things at once. Your moods are mercurial and you change your mind quickly.

Aries with Cancer Rising

You are close to your family, very home loving and also very careful with money. You may be interested in military matters and attracted to teaching or helping the weak.

Aries with Leo Rising

You may be bumptious and aggravating at times but you are great fun and a very loving and affectionate partner. You love travel and education.

Aries with Virgo Rising

You are quieter, more modest and hard-working than most Ariens. You lack confidence but you are ambitious. You are very keen on healing, psychic or investigative matters.

Aries with Libra Rising

You are much more laid back than the average Arien and you wait for other people to motivate you. You are good looking with a sexy, charismatic personality.

Aries with Scorpio Rising

You have a powerhouse personality, being a really hard worker and go-getter who won't let anything stand in your way. You could be very keen on the military, police or engineering work.

Aries with Sagittarius Rising

You are a true pioneer, an adventurer with very itchy feet. You could take up a very glamorous job or something wonderful like being a comedian or a top ballet dancer.

Aries with Capricorn Rising

You are a very powerful personality who wants to reach the top and this may compensate you for a difficult childhood.

Aries with Aquarius Rising

You have a funny attitude towards money and goods, possibly amassing them and then giving them away again. You value education and you have a clever, inventive mind.

Aries with Pisces Rising

You may be quiet, shy and nondescript but you have a powerfully self-centred ambition. You could choose an artistic, sporting or glamorous way of life.

Aries in 1995

Signs and Symbols

The table at the beginning of each month shows your
general trends for the month ahead. The symbols are very
easy to understand because the hearts show the state of your
love life, the stars tell you how your work is likely to go, the
dollar signs tell you whether this will be a good month for
money, the heartbeat graphs show your general health and
energy levels and the horse shoes tell you whether this will
be a lucky month or not.

The Aspects and their Astrological Meanings

CONJUNCT This shows important events which are usually,
  but not always, good.

SEXTILE Good, particularly for work and mental activity.

SQUARE Difficult, challenging.

TRINE Great for romance, family life and creativity.

OPPOSITE Awkward, depressing, challenging.

INTO This shows when a particular planet enters a new
  sign of the zodiac, thus setting off a new phase or
  a new set of circumstances.

January at a Glance

LOVE	♥	♥	♥	♥	♥
WORK	★	★	★		
MONEY	$	$	$	$	
FITNESS	◓				
LUCK	U	U	U		

Sunday, 1st January
Moon conjunct Sun

If there was ever a start to a year of ambition . . . this is it!
The New Moon in your fellow cardinal sign of Capricorn
encourages you to take an ambitious stance at the start of
'95. As you know, Aries is the sign of new beginnings so
you're no stranger to New Year resolutions. Now, you're
determined to reach the top, to make your mark on the
professional world . . . and woe betide any who stand in
your way or try to slow you down with distractions and petty
irrelevances. You may be considering a career change. If
that's the case, then you have the energy and initiative to
achieve your aims. It's a forceful New Year's Day for you!

Monday, 2nd January
Mercury conjunct Neptune

After yesterday's upward and onward thrust of ambition,
you're quite likely to be having second thoughts today. The
rational processes that are the gift of Mercury are dimmed

in the confusing influence of Neptune. You may feel that all your high-flown aims are just too much for you to cope with. Now Aries is a sign that generally has no shortage of self-confidence, so hold to your course. You can be sure it's the right thing.

Tuesday, 3rd January
Moon sextile Jupiter

There's no doubt that you are determined to improve your position as far as professional success and standing are concerned, but of course, you may feel that some improvement of the mind is also in order. Perhaps a new educational course at an evening class would appeal now. You're such a determined person, that you should dismiss any idea that it would be a waste of time. Remember that the energy you expend now will be amply repaid with achievement.

Wednesday, 4th January
Mercury conjunct Uranus

When Mercury and Uranus mingle their influences you can be sure that it's going to be a day for inspiration. Good news is on its way that will literally revolutionize your way of thinking. It's almost as if a metaphorical light bulb has lit up in your head casting out all confusions and providing solutions to long-standing problems. Be prepared to entertain unusual or even eccentric thoughts and suggestions. After the helter-skelter whirlwind of today's stars there are few complications that can hold you back.

Thursday, 5th January
Mercury sextile Venus

Since you're obviously in a go-ahead mood it'd be far too easy to impulsively race ahead without a thought for anyone else. Yet there is something to be said for making time to chat with a valued friend or colleague. Subtlety is the key to advancement today since a small hint could open up a whole new panorama of experience. Use some charm now and you're likely to learn something to your advantage.

Friday, 6th January
Mercury into Aquarius

The swiftly moving planet Mercury enters the sign of Aquarius today and gives a remarkable uplift to your social prospects. From now until 14th March you'll find yourself at the centre point of friendly interactions. People will seek you out for the pleasure of your company. It's also a good time to get in contact with distant friends and those you haven't seen for a while. The only fly in the ointment is that you shouldn't expect a small phone bill.

Saturday, 7th January
Venus into Sagittarius

Mercury's obviously set a fashion, because today Venus too changes sign, though in her case it's your fellow fire sign of Sagittarius. Since she also meets up with Pluto this is definitely an indication of adventure! The old, the tried and true, the familiar have absolutely no appeal now. You'll get the sense the future is out there waiting for you, and typically you'll be impatient to get to it. This exciting planetary influence lasts until 4th February so make the most of it.

Sunday, 8th January
Moon trine Jupiter

With the added encouragement of Jupiter in your house of adventure and travel, the Moon urges movement in your life. This is not a day to sit at home knitting. Get out and about, meet people, go sightseeing. In short, anything that gives a new experience is favoured now. If you don't feel that you can just take off, then open a good book or watch an interesting documentary. The mind needs some expansion so give it the chance.

Monday, 9th January
Moon square Uranus

The desire for the new in your life proves something of a mixed blessing today because the harsh angle between the Moon and Uranus sets up a grumble of dissatisfaction that could last the day through. Nothing seems right, fast enough or exciting enough to suit you. I know it's a Monday but the blues really have you in their grip. Try to develop a little patience, it'll help.

Tuesday, 10th January
Venus square Mars

Yesterday's dissatisfied stars continue I'm afraid. This time it's the fault of Venus at loggerheads with your ruler, Mars. Though you can think of nothing more pleasurable than travel and excitement now, the call of duty is very strong indeed so you'll be irritated by the demands placed on you by others, and by the actual routine of your life. All I can do is again urge patience, otherwise that fiery temper will flare.

Wednesday, 11th January
Moon trine Sun

At last that terrible restlessness is under control. As the Moon harmoniously links with the Sun a contentment and calmness overtakes your mood. You'll feel as if you're getting somewhere, and that the next stages are obvious. This happier atmosphere may have something to do with a small financial boost that should turn up very soon.

Thursday, 12th January
Moon opposite Pluto

Aries people are quite often selfish . . . . I know you don't mean to be, but you can get so caught up in your own desires and aims that you tend to forget that others too have aspirations and needs. Today is a case in point: the situation must have got out of control in recent days because you are the subject of heavy-handed hints and possibly some emotional blackmail. All someone close really wants is some attention. If you want an easy life, then affectionately provide it.

Friday, 13th January
Moon trine Mercury

Though this is supposed to be an ill-omened day, the stars have a completely different message. In fact, messages and communications of all kinds are highlighted now. Good news, pleasant companionship and hassle-free travel will make this a memorable time. Sometimes it's just good to be alive. It's obvious that you are well thought of because friends will be happy to express their regard and good wishes.

Saturday, 14th January
Sun conjunct Neptune

Other people's problems are the main feature of today. You'll be called upon to provide tea, sympathy and possibly a box of tissues to a friend who needs someone to talk to. OK, I know you're not the ideal candidate but take some time out to show that you at least do care. If work worries or frustrations are at the root of this, you'll at least have an instinctive sense of the way things will go.

Sunday, 15th January
Venus conjunct Jupiter

A conjunction of the two beneficial planets Venus and Jupiter must herald a fortunate day. When this occurs in the area of adventure and travel, it's obvious that the attraction of foreign cultures and far-off places is the order of the day. It's also a time to be friendly: show kindness even to strangers now because the smallest gesture of concern will be amply repaid. It's a day to take the wider view and not get bogged down in details.

Monday, 16th January
Moon opposite Sun

The Full Moon in the sign of Cancer puts the lunar spotlight on all family and domestic issues. Perhaps it's time for some straight talking because this is the best opportunity you'll get to put an end to home-based or emotional problems. In some ways it's time to put your cards on the table, yet equally to give credit and take some share of blame in family affairs. Apart from such personal concerns it's time to speak to someone in authority about your ambitions.

Tuesday, 17th January
Pluto into Sagittarius

Pluto is a very slow-moving planet occupying one sign for years, even decades so when it finally does decide to change home its transit heralds a major change, which though subtle alters everything connected to the sign it's found in. Today, Pluto enters Sagittarius bringing its transformative influence to bear on your deepest beliefs and personal philosophy. You'll find yourself pondering such subjects as the meaning of life and the wonder of the universe. Travel and encounters with exotic ideas will have a profound influence on your thinking from now on.

Wednesday, 18th January
Moon trine Mercury

It's an uplifting day as you see the possibilities of moving farther afield. Your adventurous outgoing mood is infectious now, and you'll find yourself the centre of romantic attraction. Your flirtatious attitude will find ready admirers. This is an excellent time to make travel plans and generally add to your social circle. There's amusement and interesting information to be gained from a child or younger person.

Thursday, 19th January
Mars square Pluto

Nagging discontent is the source of any health problem as you must admit if you're going to feel any better. Anxiety and stress are psychological problems which can have very real physical effects. Be honest with yourself today, because facing up to unpleasant facts is the first step in overcoming them. You're in need of some tender loving care now.

Friday, 20th January
Sun into Aquarius

As the Sun makes its yearly entrance into Aquarius, you can be sure that friends and acquaintances are going to have a powerful influence on your prospects. The Sun's harmonious angle to your own sign gives an optimism and vitality to your outgoing nature. Social life will increase in importance over the next month. You'll be a popular and much sought-after person. Obstacles that have irritated you will now be swept away.

Saturday, 21st January
Moon square Venus

You seem prone to minor ailments at present but you've got to admit that a lot of it is your own fault. A tendency to over-indulge in the good things of life could be the culprit here. Too much rich food or alcohol isn't doing your system any favours. Try to restrain yourself today, and give your body the rest it so richly deserves.

Sunday, 22nd January
Mars into Leo

Your ruling planet, Mars has been travelling backwards through the zodiac for some time now and today reaches your fellow fire sign of Leo. Your desires suddenly become very strong indeed, and temptations will tend to sweep you up without a single thought to the consequences. If the path of true love doesn't run smooth, it's not for want of passionate intensity on your part. The one thing to watch for is that you'll tend to move so swiftly that you're prone to minor cuts and bruises . . . . Take it easy.

Monday, 23rd January
Moon sextile Mars

There's a bit more of that passionate intensity today. If you're attached then the combined influences of Mars and the Moon will blow away any of the cobwebs from your relationship. Physically, you'll be very demanding, though I doubt that there'll be many objections to that trait. Love affairs old and new are the centre of your interest now, but remember that you are rather too assertive at the moment, so try not to frighten the object of desire off before you turn out the light.

Tuesday, 24th January
Moon square Sun

You've expended so much energy recently that it's about time you cut down on all your furious activities and took it easy for a while. Your passions are very strong at the moment with all these sudden attractions racing into your life, but it's important that you take some time to think, and simply to sit down and rest. If you don't at least try some relaxation, you'll be back to a stressed out state in no time.

Wednesday, 25th January
Mercury retrograde

Today begins a period when your optimism will fall short of its usual level. It's the fault of Mercury which turns retrograde, and continues in a backwards course until 16th February. This isn't a serious problem but you must be aware that at times you will feel as if your hopes have been dashed and your faith in friends misplaced. Of course there's little substance in these feelings yet rumours in the next few weeks may be disturbing.

Thursday, 26th January
Moon square Mars

Today's irritable aspect between the Moon and Mars puts you in an edgy mood; perhaps you'll have an early encounter with someone out of sorts. Other people's anxieties have got a way of rubbing off on you at the moment, so if you want any peace, then try to steer clear of moaners. Controversial subjects are another no, since you never know who is going to overhear your conversation.

Friday, 27th January
Moon conjunct Venus

In total contrast to yesterday's tense aspect, today's stars promise nothing but harmony and contentment. The Moon makes a splendid contact with Venus this Friday and bestows the ability to enjoy life to its fullest. Any past family difficulties, such as rows with in-laws can now be put behind you and oil poured on troubled waters. You'll feel at one with the world.

Saturday, 28th January
Mercury sextile Venus

You'll have plenty of opportunity to show off your wit and wisdom today for as you warm to your pet subject you'll entrance those around you with verbal dexterity. If an amusing companion is required then no one need look any further than you. People you meet today will rapidly become friends because your open, honest charm is very appealing.

Sunday, 29th January
Moon sextile Saturn

There's plenty to occupy your time this Sunday as you get to grips with a thousand and one neglected chores. Of course, normally you wouldn't be so keen to organize yourself so thoroughly but you fancy an orderly start to the new week. You're in a practical mood determined that there's a place for everything, and everything should be in its place.

Monday, 30th January
Moon conjunct Sun

There's no doubt that issues surrounding friendship and trust are very important now. The New Moon in your horoscopic area of social activities ensures that encounters with interesting people will yield new and enduring friendships. Though your mood has tended to vary between optimism and despair recently, the new Moon can't fail to increase your confidence and vitality.

Tuesday, 31st January
Sun sextile Jupiter

It may be a Tuesday but social life and celebrations should still be the central attraction. It doesn't matter if you have to travel some distance to meet up with your friends because the journey will be worth it. You may even see another, fascinating side to someone you thought you knew well. A profound expression of wisdom will renew your interest.

February at a Glance

LOVE	♥				
WORK	★	★	★	★	
MONEY	$	$			
FITNESS	(◐)	(◐)	(◐)	(◐)	
LUCK	♘	♘			

Wednesday, 1st February
Moon opposite Mars

When an Aries gets on a high horse there's no sign to beat you. All that fiery Martial energy is pouring out in one great flood. If you see the slightest hint of injustice today, your reaction will be furious as you prepare to stand up for the rights of others. The bigger they are, the harder they fall, that's your attitude now because this Wednesday, you'll relish the challenge!

Thursday, 2nd February
Venus trine Mars

A romantic atmosphere prevails today as Mars and Venus inspire love divine. Unattached Ariens are prone to sudden attraction, and wild infatuation today, while those who are already linked should take advantage of the passionate vibes to rekindle some of the old magic in your relationship. A trip to a memorable location could play a part in affairs of the heart now.

Friday, 3rd February
Moon square Venus

After yesterday's romantically hopeful stars, the harsh angle between the Moon and Venus shows self-doubt creeping in now. It's a fact that after euphoria there often follows a sense of anti-climax and that's the case today. Pull yourself together, all is well and this hopeless mood will fade if you give yourself space to be calm.

Saturday, 4th February
Venus into Capricorn

Venus, the goddess of love and growth passes into your fellow cardinal sign of Capricorn today, ensuring that the next few weeks will be a time of progress and advancement in your career area. The planet boosts that well-hidden capacity of diplomacy enabling you to get your own way without confrontation. Social affairs and out of office meetings may well prove advantageous.

Sunday, 5th February
Moon square Uranus

And I thought Sunday was supposed to be a day of rest! . . . No such luck, I'm afraid, for the tense aspect between the Moon and Uranus causes a lot of disruption to your peace of mind. It could be that you are carrying far too many work worries home, or the burden of an elderly relative is proving too pressing to give any peace. Fretting doesn't work so try to approach problems in a calmer frame of mind.

Monday, 6th February
Moon trine Mars, square Venus

It's a mixed bag of fortunes for Monday. Though you've got energy aplenty, the more emotional side of life looks fraught with anxiety. It could be that you are actually doing an excellent job, yet feel as if you could do better. The creative side of your personality certainly shines, but the variable Aries self-confidence is equally shaken. Try to stand back and take a realistic look at your potentials.

Tuesday, 7th February
Mercury sextile Jupiter

The normal routine of life holds little appeal today for Jupiter and Mercury stimulate an interest far away from your usual activities. If you get the chance, then travel. Both these planets open doorways of opportunity for fun, new experience and adventure. If you can drag a friend along, so much the better because you'll enjoy the company as much as the sight-seeing.

Wednesday, 8th February
Moon square Mars

Any spare cash will burn a hole in your pocket this Wednesday because you'll be set on a spending spree of outrageous extravagance. It's not the necessities you need worry about, but the more useless an item, the more you'll want it. In some ways this is actually a reaction to too much thrift in your life, but still, try to hold back when your purchasing power isn't that great.

Thursday, 9th February
Moon trine Mercury

As the Moon makes harmonious contact with the eloquent Mercury you can be sure of some charming distractions, and even welcome disruptions to routine. Friends pop in and phone constantly providing a witty and amusing barrage of gossip and trivia. Laughter and pleasant company are just the tonic you need.

Friday, 10th February
Moon sextile Mars

It seems that the theme for the end of this week is fun. Today, the Moon and your ruler, Mars continue the social trend, mixing in a little romantic passion for good measure. This is a day to circulate amongst people you like and respect. You never know, but a friendship may deepen into something more intimate before very long.

Saturday, 11th February
Moon opposite Venus

After a couple of frivolous days, you may think that you can have too much of a good thing. It's not that you're back to earth with a bump, yet you're now keen to get back to more mundane pastimes and duties. It's time to catch up on neglected chores simply to take your mind off some sensitive issues in your life. Even you realize it's a good thing to have your feet on the ground.

Sunday, 12th February
Sun opposite Mars

This is one where the fire of the Aries temper is too close to the surface for comfort. The wrong word could get a reaction far out of proportion to the offence. Humour is distinctly thin on the ground now, and woe betide anyone who makes light of a serious issue around you! Lazy people too are likely to irritate you to distraction . . . even if it is Sunday!

Monday, 13th February
Moon opposite Uranus

The disturbing ripples of yesterday's irritations are given an unexpected twist by the Moon's opposition to Uranus now. This is one of those days when you feel frustrated and surrounded by other people's petty obstacles.

Independence and a freedom to do your own thing is vital now, and you could be quite forceful in making sure that's exactly what you get. It's too easy to ride roughshod over other's feelings today.

Tuesday, 14th February
Moon trine Jupiter

At last the thunderclouds have passed and a more convivial atmosphere takes hold as the Moon contacts Jupiter, spreading a little happiness around you. Negative moods are now forgiven and forgotten as harmonious influences lift your spirits. Since it is St Valentine's Day, you could make a special effort to show the more romantic side to your nature and take some time out for an intimate celebration to remember.

Wednesday, 15th February
Moon opposite Sun

Today's Full Moon occurs in your solar house of pleasure, leisure, romance and children bringing these areas of your life into sharp focus. You may be called upon to take a realistic view of a love affair that seems to be going nowhere . . . and think again. A choice awaits you there. Equally, a younger person may need your guidance and support while going through a difficult period.

Thursday, 16th February
Mercury direct

If you've not been seeing eye to eye with certain friends recently, you can put the blame on Mercury's wayward course which has made all social relations that much more difficult recently. Fortunately, the tiny planet is now moving along the right road so it's time to pour oil on troubled waters and re-establish the friendly social links you previously enjoyed.

Friday, 17th February
Moon trine Uranus

The temptation to over-indulge in good food and drink is very strong today, but you've got to admit that the winter period has taken its toll on your physical state. It's high time that you took the whole subject of your health a little more seriously. Many Aries people should be considering a new healthy diet, while others need seriously to think about taking more exercise.

Saturday, 18th February
Moon trine Mercury

With Mercury now in direct motion it's time to get hold of friends and associates. This should be a tremendously social day full of exchanges of views and even some intellectual argument. The important thing is that everyone should know where they stand, especially in your affections. With such eloquent stars, you should be able to express your true feelings most convincingly.

Sunday, 19th February
Sun into Pisces

A certain depth is added to your straightforward character when the Sun moves into your solar house of mystery and the unconscious mind. Deep drives and motivations are beginning to stir and probe towards the surface. As the Sun moves through Pisces it gives you an unparalleled chance to come to terms with any old guilts, regrets and anxieties that have plagued you. It's a sort of psychological spring clean until 21st March.

Monday, 20th February
Sun square Pluto

It's as if the Sun has decided to force the issue of psychological cleansing by getting into a tussle with Pluto at the start of this week. You're questioning everything! Daily habits, established pathways, cherished beliefs . . . . Nothing is sacred! You really want to know if you're clinging to outmoded thoughts or practices. One thing is sure: this celestial wrestling match will be worth it no matter how uncomfortable it is now.

Tuesday, 21st February
Moon sextile Venus

The link between the Moon and Venus adds a compelling and seductive quality to your nature now. Since you're quick on the uptake, it won't take you long to realize that you're in a position to twist anyone around your little finger. A small flirtation today will gain you far more than any number of confrontations.

Wednesday, 22nd February
Moon square Sun

There's a touch of over-sensitivity about you today. I know you can usually brazen out unpleasant encounters, but just at the moment, you'd far rather completely avoid awkward situations and people. Actually this is a good thing at the moment, so don't try to force yourself into any actions that you aren't completely happy with. Being assertive could hurt your interests just now.

Thursday, 23rd February
Moon trine Mars

With your sensitivity a little more under control, you're back to being an exciting soul today. It wouldn't take much for you to take off in search of some adventure. So much the better if you can find an amusing companion to share in the experience. This could turn out to be an extremely romantic interlude.

Friday, 24th February
Moon into Capricorn

Though you'd probably never admit it, you're very conscious of your public image, and as the Moon transits the sign of Capricorn, you'll feel a craving for admiration. More importantly perhaps, you'll need respect to be shown you. Of course, desires aren't always fulfilled, so if you are to avoid a black mood by the end of the day, hold back on expressing opinions too forcefully. Don't try too hard, and let the real you shine through.

Saturday, 25th February
Moon conjunct Venus

The Moon's conjunction with Venus ensures an atmosphere of affection today. I'm sure you'll admit that a little understanding goes a long way so it's important that you make time to show that you care now. If a colleague or working acquaintance is in need of sympathy then make sure that you supply it. You never know, it could do your prospects some good.

Sunday, 26th February
Venus conjunct Neptune

At last a restful day! You know you could do with one so it's with a sigh of relief that the rays of Venus and Neptune combine to provide an aura of gentle affection. You'll gratefully realize how much someone close has sacrificed to aid your ambitions. Their selfless acts should now be repaid with a demonstration of your love.

Monday, 27th February
Moon opposite Mars

After such a sentimental weekend, you feel ready to take on the world and win now. Of course there are still practical obstacles to be overcome but you've got all the drive, energy and bloody-minded determination you could ever need to defeat them. It's a good thing you are independent because those around you provide little help now. Self-reliance is the key to success today.

Tuesday, 28th February
Moon square Pluto

There's no point in taking anything at face value today, not unless you want to be ripped off or otherwise messed about. You really need to keep your wits about you and carefully analyse any bits of information that come your way. If thinking of travel, then take care, for as we all know attractive brochures can be extremely misleading.

March at a Glance

LOVE	♥	♥			
WORK	★				
MONEY	$	$	$		
FITNESS	⊗	⊗	⊗	⊗	
LUCK	♘	♘	♘	♘	

Wednesday, 1st March
Moon conjunct Sun

March begins most aptly with a New Moon, strongly affecting your most private thoughts. The whole inner world of imagination is highlighted now, allowing you to sort out priorities, to ditch old, worn-out obsessions and put your psychological self into a clearer, more healthy state. Privacy will tend to be an important issue today, so if you can, a period of withdrawal from the rat race would be most beneficial.

Thursday, 2nd March
Venus into Aquarius

Social life, friendships and a general sense of optimism and wonder are due today as Venus enters your solar house of hope and platonic affection. Until the 28th of this month there will be an ease and understanding with those you deal with. Friends will provide the reassurance and affection that you need at the moment. Your own personal charm too is on a high, while women in your life take on a more important role.

Friday, 3rd March
Venus sextile Pluto

Though you still tend to be deep in thought, the company of those special people who think so highly of you is a very important part of the process now. There are stirrings of a need to break free of all restrictions, and if you make the effort to enquire, you'll find that your friends feel the same way too. Why not plan a change of scene with favoured friends. It'll do you the world of good.

Saturday, 4th March
Pluto retrograde

All the philosophizing you've been indulging in for the last couple of days is certainly showing signs of transforming some of your deepest convictions as Pluto takes a backward step today. The planet's presence in Sagittarius has given you a taste of things to come, showing the freedom and wealth of experience that awaits you. Of course there are practical matters to be considered now, and you'd do well to deal carefully with the nitty gritty financial side of your life for some months to come.

Sunday, 5th March
Moon square Venus

It's obvious that you don't appreciate interruption at the moment, no matter how well meaning, but you'll only blame yourself if you let fly with that hot Arien temper today. You're sorting out your feelings and tend to be over sensitive now – but don't be too hard on yourself. Those who know you well, do understand your little faults as well as your good side.

Monday, 6th March
Sun square Jupiter

If, like the rest of us, you feel that Monday is an unwelcome jolt of reality, the Sun's square aspect to Jupiter can only make this feeling worse. The day to day duties expected of you seem far too heavy a burden. The smallest task becomes a mammoth bind, taking you away from the flights of imagination of your inner world. Don't build molehills into mountains today . . . . And just take it as it comes.

Tuesday, 7th March
Sun conjunct Saturn

It's getting more obvious that all your well-meaning intentions and appreciation of your life's potential isn't cutting any ice with the grim practicalities of day to day existence. You've got to get down to detail and sort out some pressing matters before you can possibly create your ideal world. I know it's boring, yet very necessary if you're to make the most of the more expansive messages coming from your chart.

Wednesday, 8th March
Moon trine Venus

Yesterday's drudgery can go hang as far as you're concerned now. The Moon makes a splendid aspect to Venus which puts you in a rather frivolous and very sociable frame of mind. You feel a need to go out, visit friends and indulge in the pleasures of conversation. Go with the flow today, and give in to your desires . . . . They seem innocent enough.

Thursday, 9th March
Moon trine Mercury

Get a hold of that Aries impulsiveness today, because the intellectually stimulating stars encourage the triumph of planning and brains. This is an excellent time to get in contact with those you haven't seen in ages. Who knows, old friends may be falling over themselves to get in touch with you.

Friday, 10th March
Mars trine Jupiter

There's a tremendous boost to your physical and mental energies today as your ruling planet Mars enters a superb angle with the expansive Jupiter. Optimism, vivacity and a lust for life are the gifts of this powerful stellar influence. You'll be outgoing, exuberant and playful now. Both the romantic area of your life and travel affairs will benefit.

Saturday, 11th March
Moon trine Saturn

If ever there was a day to stick close to your home patch, this is it! With the Moon and Saturn putting such an emphasis on privacy and comfort, you'd be doing yourself no favours if you strayed too far. Put your feet up and relax if you can possibly contain your impulsive nature. If not, then potter around catching up on all those neglected chores around the house.

Sunday, 12th March
Moon opposite Uranus

It's always a time for the unexpected when the planet Uranus casts an unpredictable aura over your family. Perhaps the fault actually lies with you since events far away from your home could put you in an irritable mood, which you're quite likely to take out on those close. Try to keep a cool head.

Monday, 13th March
Moon opposite Venus

Though you may have to give your prospects a kick start this week, the stellar message is one of creativity and potential. You feel in a particularly artistic mood now, and are appreciative of painting, music and more cultural pursuits. Unfortunately, both children and friends tend to be quite demanding, so your enlightening idyll will be short lived or occur in bursts.

Tuesday, 14th March
Mercury into Pisces

Though you've been in quite a philosophical and introspective mood for some time now, the passage of Mercury into your solar house of psychology and sensitivity adds a more rational influence to this area of your life. At last you'll be able to understand the deep emotional processes that have been occurring. A more reclusive, private mood will appeal until the start of April. By the end of this period you should understand yourself much better.

Wednesday, 15th March
Mercury square Pluto

There's more than a touch of paranoia about Ariens this Wednesday. Of course you're still in the introspective phase and any disruption of your thought processes will result in your feeling as though you are being picked on. There's not much point in explaining that this isn't the case since you aren't in a reasonable frame of mind. Try not to jump to conclusions.

Thursday, 16th March
Sun sextile Neptune

The mood lifts today as the Sun and Neptune reach harmonious agreement. Your imagination is boosted and your intuition is on top form. In business matters this is an excellent influence since you can feel your way through problems without allowing them to upset your equilibrium. Of course there is no shortage of peculiar tasks to occupy your time, but if you follow your hunches all will be well.

Friday, 17th March
Moon opposite Sun

The Full Moon in Virgo encourages you to take a good look at the state of your health. Are there any nasty little habits that aren't doing you any good? I'm willing to bet that there are! Apart from that, the whole work situation comes under scrutiny too. If you aren't satisfied with your day to day activities, it's time to look around for something more fulfilling.

Saturday, 18th March
Moon sextile Mars

This fairly long-lasting state of introspection may be good for you but close partnerships may have been suffering from inadvertent neglect. Today's aspect between the Moon and Mars gives you a chance to remedy that situation. If you're honest you'll agree that both of you are in need of some excitement to add a little spice to your relationship.

Sunday, 19th March
Moon square Uranus

Your Sundays are rarely uneventful at the moment and today's no exception. The Moon challenges Uranus to make this one of the most unpredictable and eccentric days you've had in ages. Be prepared for the worm to turn now and the most timorous person to display an unsuspected forceful side to their character. Though peace is unlikely, if you want any then steer clear of controversy.

Monday, 20th March
Sun sextile Uranus

Nothing is as it seems this Monday. A fresh insight will be gained into the most ordinary areas of your life as the Sun makes a positive aspect to Uranus. Uranus's influence today is an extremely beneficial one, removing obstacles, opening up career possibilities and granting you an originality that would be hard to beat. Invention should be your watchword now. Don't be afraid of the new!

Tuesday, 21st March
Sun into Aries

Today is the Spring Equinox when the Sun moves into your own sign. This time of year is the start of an upswing for you granting an increase in confidence and vitality. You may consider that it's the perfect opportunity for a change of image just in time for your birthday. The solar force smiles on you, and you'll smile on the world at large . . . there's plenty to smile about!

Wednesday, 22nd March
Moon trine Mars

The positive astral influence continues today as the Moon makes a strong harmonious aspect to your ruler Mars. Now, your assertive and confident personality will combine with a natural charm ensuring that you get your own way without any confrontations. There should be plenty of fun in the offing, with just a dash of passion. You're doing pretty well!

Thursday, 23rd March
Moon sextile Venus

Traditionally, your ruling planet Mars rules the rush of adrenalin, giving you the reputation for rashness. However, that's the last thing you want today. In fact a little calm would be worth its weight in gold at the moment. Female friends will be a great comfort now, helping you to let go of tension and freeing up your emotional expression.

Friday, 24th March
Mars direct

Mars has occupied your solar house of leisure, play and romance for some time now, but it has been rolling backwards too. From today, as your ruling planet resumes direct motion, all issues connected with your passions should go better. Any frustrations you've laboured under will fade away giving more satisfaction to your life. In short, fun times are here again!

Saturday, 25th March
Mercury square Jupiter

The harsh aspect between Mercury and Jupiter casts the often uncomfortable light of reality into the darkest recesses of your imagination. Unreal dreams will be ruthlessly set aside as you get a much needed dose of common sense. This needn't be depressing at all, it just keeps your feet on the ground. The only danger to watch for is that you'll tend to be caught out if you lie or exaggerate.

Sunday, 26th March
Mercury conjunct Saturn

Secrets and confidences are the main theme of Friday's stars. If you're the one who finds that keeping up a cloak of concealment is a terrible strain on the nerves, then be prepared to share the dreadful facts with someone close. I think you'll find that it's not so dreadful after all, and will be surprised at the understanding you receive. They say that confession is good for the soul.

Monday, 27th March
Moon conjunct Venus

It may be Monday but the conjunction between Venus and the Moon heralds an extremely social period. Seek out some entertainment in company with friends. It's a case of the more the merrier at the moment, and you never know, a friendship could develop a more romantic flavour by the end of this evening. This is a time to get out and meet people.

Tuesday, 28th March
Venus into Pisces

Your inner life is in harmony with events in your day to day existence at the moment, and as Venus now enters your solar house of privacy and psychic feeling a profound sense of peace enters your life. You'll instinctively know that no matter what is going on in the world, all is actually well.

Wednesday, 29th March
Venus square Pluto

Though you are often impulsive, every now and again a warning voice sounds in your inner ear preventing you from a downright stupid course of action. That's the way it is today as Venus and Pluto join forces to divert you from the crooked path. The road to hell is said to be paved with good intentions; it's a good thing you've got enough common sense to recognize when you're taking the wrong turn.

Thursday, 30th March
Mercury sextile Neptune

The planet Neptune is associated with inspiration and poetry, so when it mingles its force with eloquent Mercury it's excellent for the expression of your deepest feelings. Rational thought and mystical intuition work together now. However, in practical or work affairs you may cause a lot of confusion if you try to communicate your insights. Your dreams could take on added meaning.

Friday, 31st March
Moon conjunct Sun

The month ends with a New Moon in your own sign. This is a powerfully positive influence that encourages you to make a new start. Personal opportunities are about to change your life. You must now be prepared to leave the past behind to embark on a brand new course. Decide what you want, because you'll be your own best guide now.

April at a Glance

LOVE	♥	♥	♥		
WORK	★	★	★		
MONEY	$	$	$	$	
FITNESS	〰	〰	〰		
LUCK	U	U	U	U	U

Saturday, 1st April
Jupiter retrograde, Uranus into Aquarius

Jupiter turns backward today, and since that planet can be considered the joker of the planetary deck, makes an apt influence for April Fool's Day. Keep your feet on the ground and remember that just because the general outlook is good for you personally doesn't mean that you don't have to work for it; it won't be handed to you on a plate. In many ways you have to make your own luck at the moment, but even so educational and travel matters may meet with delays and frustrations for a while. On a happier note, the planet Uranus enters your house of social activity and friendship today so you'll have all the backing you need to keep you on course.

Sunday, 2nd April
Mercury into Aries

It seems to be the time for major planetary movements for Mercury races into your own sign now, giving you not only an eloquent tongue, but the opportunity to express your ideas and inspirations clearly and persuasively. You have a busy period up until the 17th of this month, with constant letters and phone calls bringing gossip, laughs and fascinating information your way.

Monday, 3rd April
Moon trine Neptune

Though today brings a good aspect between the Moon and Neptune your financial situation is prone to deceptive influences. This is not a day when you should be prepared to sign on the dotted line, because you'll be too vague to take much notice of the small print. More generally, you will have a sense of the rightness of your professional course.

Tuesday, 4th April
Sun trine Mars

You're a regular dynamo this Tuesday! The powerful positive influences of the Sun and Mars give you enormous energy and enthusiasm. You're in the mood for fun and will throw yourself heart and soul into any activity that takes your fancy. Artistic talent, romance and any and all creative potentials should flourish.

Wednesday, 5th April
Moon square Saturn

As if in reaction to yesterday's marvellous stars, you've gone into a despondent mood now. It's too easy to be pessimistic today, but you should remember that every cloud's got a silver lining, and it's mainly a matter of your frame of mind. Console yourself with the thought that the general outlook is good, so do try to smile.

Thursday, 6th April
Sun trine Jupiter

Aries people have restless feet today. The prospect of the coming summer opens your eyes to everything that the world has to offer. You want to be up and away as soon as possible so this should be an excellent time to make plans for a much needed holiday. Friends who are far away may come into your thoughts now, so perhaps you should get in touch.

Friday, 7th April
Moon trine Venus

Nostalgia rules the day as far as you're concerned now. It doesn't take much of a stimulus, a familiar song, a phrase or a waft of perfume to set you on the road to remembrance. Why don't you give in to the sentimental mood and dig out an old photograph album to relive some of the happiest days of your life.

Saturday, 8th April
Moon opposite Neptune

Though you're feeling reasonably secure, the same might not be said for some of your relations. Over sensitivity and over reaction are likely now, and try as you might, there'll be some difficulty in calming family members down. Of course, by the end of this trying time you may be over wrought emotionally too so you'll need a peaceful home environment to relax in.

Sunday, 9th April
Mercury trine Mars

Aries is known as the pioneer of the zodiac, and today's stars give you the chance to prove it. You won't be content to follow blindly someone else's lead and will feel an overpowering urge to make some of your most personal opinions forcefully known. You're eloquent and persuasive now with a passion that could move mountains. Don't be afraid to stand out from the crowd this Sunday.

Monday, 10th April
Venus square Jupiter

Though you're much in demand socially, you'll be in no mood to stick to one person or topic for very long today. Those two generous planets, Venus and Jupiter successfully increase your charm but also add a wicked element of flirtation and teasing. At least this will give you a very alluring and enigmatic aura. Foreigners or news from abroad will again be a feature of the day.

Tuesday, 11th April
Mercury trine Jupiter

A mentally acute, optimistic and positive influence is at work today. As Mercury joins with Jupiter, your rational processes are working like lightning. It's your chance to express the wealth of experience and wisdom that you've gained over the years. Those around you will be very impressed by your abilities and breadth of knowledge.

Wednesday, 12th April
Mars trine Jupiter

'Think Big': that's the stellar message for today as your ruling planet makes a marvellous aspect to Jupiter. Your enthusiasm is boundless as you seek out mental and physical challenges to test your prowess. This is an extremely fortunate day in which you should set yourself goals, and be sure that you have the ability to achieve them.

Thursday, 13th April
Venus conjunct Saturn

It's obvious that you're preoccupied with your own big plans this Thursday since those who are special to you think that you're being rather distant and cool. It's all the fault of Venus, who's now in the cool embrace of Saturn. It's not that your opinions or feelings have changed, it's just that you may have a little difficulty in expressing them freely now.

Friday, 14th April
Moon sextile Mars

There's no doubt that you're in need of some independence in your life now. Of course, if you're in a partnership you can't just take off and do your own thing so some negotiation and reassurance is vital. Explain that you need some extra scope and freedom. Possessiveness is hard to bear now, but remember that your other half may be feeling insecure.

Saturday, 15th April
Mercury square Neptune

It's definitely going to be a confusing day when Mercury is in hard aspect to misty Neptune. Since Mercury governs the thought processes, the vague, bewildering influence of Neptune seems to pack your mind in cotton wool. It's not the best day for making financial commitments, or indeed entering any important agreements at all. Don't make big decisions, and put off legal or money matters until you feel more mentally together.

Sunday, 16th April
Sun square Neptune

The Neptunian influence continues on Easter Sunday as the Sun's strength is sapped by the influence of that misty planet. Take it easy today. You desperately need some harmony and peace to take your mind off professional worries. Try not to let your fears run away with you now. Have a lazy day because you deserve one.

Monday, 17th April
Mercury into Taurus

The mental focus is back on course today as Mercury moves into your solar house of finance and possessions. You've got until 2nd May to get your monetary life in order. You're very shrewd with cash now so you should turn your attention to ways of making some considerable profit. Of course, you should really expect quick results but wheels set in motion now will have a long-term benefit.

Tuesday, 18th April
Venus sextile Neptune

The Neptunian influence is back, but that's no cause for alarm. Now, Venus harmoniously contacts the dreamy planet filtering a sense of peace and contentment into your mental world. It's not a day for frantic activity, so slow down and allow yourself to absorb some restful planetary rays. You'll be able to function well, though you shouldn't rush at anything just now.

Wednesday, 19th April
Moon trine Sun

Yesterday must have been a refreshing experience because you're ready for anything now. The self-belief is restored and you'll relish some tough mental challenges. Ariens whose eyes are set on foreign climes again get a boost to your travel fortunes; in fact, anything that expands mental horizons is favoured. All should go well on such an auspicious day.

Thursday, 20th April
Sun into Taurus

As the Sun moves into your horoscopic area of money and possessions, it provides a welcome boost to your earning ability and general financial well being. Of course a solar movement implies much more than mere cash. Your own inner sense of values will now be explored and you'll find out exactly how much you value yourself and all you have gained so far. You can't fail to do well.

Friday, 21st April
Pluto into Scorpio

Still on a financial theme, Pluto re-enters Scorpio today, just to make sure that you've sorted out all the intimate and investment issues that have needed attention. Pluto will remain in Scorpio until 10th November, so you can expect this time to bring out issues of taxation, insurance and investments as well as more intimate sexual matters. Don't be embarrassed by anything, since this could be a heaven-sent chance to sort out long-standing problems.

Saturday, 22nd April
Venus into Aries

To help you out with your love life, Venus enters your sign today. Any problems you've had in expressing your affectionate feelings should now fade. Love is reborn in your life and you'll be generally happier and more optimistic. Another symptom of Venus in Aries, is, of course, vanity! You'll have more than your fair share of that in the next couple of weeks so a refurbished image might be in order.

Sunday, 23rd April
Venus trine Pluto

You really have entered a passionate phase. Venus, planet of love, stirs up strong sexual feelings as she makes passionate contact with Pluto today. This should be a steamy Sunday. However, for those for whom physical gymnastics hold little appeal, those passions may assume a more spiritual dimension.

Monday, 24th April
Moon square Pluto

The strange actions of a friend could arouse your suspicions today. Though you don't like to think the worst, your instincts are actually on course, and there probably is something lurking at the back of furtive actions. Of course, your curiosity is aroused now and you won't rest until you're at the bottom of this mystery.

Tuesday, 25th April
Moon conjunct Saturn

It's obviously a day for deep thinking when the Moon conjuncts Saturn in your solar house of psychology. There's no guessing what's going on in your mind now. The only danger here is that you tend to dwell on the more negative aspects of your life while ignoring the happy things. If you find yourself blowing your problems out of proportion seek out a friend for a chat. A problem shared is a problem halved.

Wednesday, 26th April
Moon trine Pluto

Though there are a lot of puzzles surrounding you just now, the Moon and Pluto encourage you to dig beneath the obvious to find the true cause of all confusions. Monetary matters, taxation affairs and anything to do with your intimate life come under scrutiny now. Keep persevering and you will turn up some satisfying answers.

Thursday, 27th April
Mercury sextile Saturn

Financial obstacles that have faced you are starting to look as though they won't be a problem for long. Some words of advice from a trustworthy person will put your monetary position in a far more positive light. A realistic, but not depressive attitude will work wonders for both your confidence and your cashflow.

Friday, 28th April
Sun conjunct Venus

The light at the end of the financial tunnel that was promised by yesterday's stars, now beams into your life with full force. You're in the right mental state to make some sensible decisions concerning the monetary realities. A plan to increase your profitability should be embraced today because the combined influences of the Sun and Venus promise considerable economic gain. Don't let this positive influence go to your head though, because you'll still tend to overspend.

Saturday, 29th April
Moon conjunct Sun

Today's solar eclipse strongly effects your money area. It does give the chance for you to develop a new perspective and direction. The eclipse will clear the air of any problems you've had in your financial fortunes, though you must be prepared to let go of old, worn-out schemes and turn your attention to more profitable means of earning. Keep an open mind now.

Sunday, 30th April
Mercury trine Neptune

Mercury is often referred to as the planet of cunning, and that trait is subtly enhanced by Neptune this Sunday. Not much can get past your beady gaze now. The direct route isn't always the one that promises the greatest success, so be prepared for some detours and by-ways on your road to the top.

May at a Glance

LOVE	♥	♥	♥	♥	♥
WORK	★	★	★	★	★
MONEY	$	$	$	$	$
FITNESS	〰	〰	〰		
LUCK	∪	∪	∪		

Monday, 1st May
Moon opposite Pluto

You've got money on the brain at the moment. Whether it's just a matter of making the domestic budget balance or you're into the high-flown world of mega millions the message is just the same. The fact that your emotional state is somewhat intense too isn't doing anything for your stress levels. Try to keep as calm as possible, and certainly not over-react to anything.

Tuesday, 2nd May
Mercury into Gemini

The Aries brain should be firing on all cylinders from today for Mercury, planet of the mind enters its own sign of Gemini. This should be the start of a highly active and social phase for you. The accent is on communication now, the clearer the better. If you've any brothers or sisters you haven't heard from in a while, why not give them a ring and renew the contact. Short journeys for business or pleasure will be favourable.

Wednesday, 3rd May
Mercury trine Uranus

The splendid aspect between rational Mercury and inspired Uranus gives a boost to all your mental processes now. A sudden surprise or some welcome news is on its way. There could be a revolution in your way of thinking as old restrictions are swept away and you'll be free to pursue your aims. Perhaps some electronic wizardry comes into this somewhere. Be prepared to accept the new in your life.

Thursday, 4th May
Venus trine Jupiter

It can't fail to be a lucky day when there's such an excellent angle between Jupiter and Venus. These two fortunate planets cast their helpful influence over travel and a deepening of understanding. A love affair that starts now has the most favourable chances possible. Be adventurous now and get out into the world, there's nothing at all to fear.

Friday, 5th May
Uranus retrograde

After a good few days, you can't expect steady progress to go too far. Uranus turns retrograde today ready for his re-entry into Capricorn, and that may give you a momentary doubt about the feasibility of many of your hopes. Friends aren't that helpful just now either, so you have to rely on your own inner reserves of strength for a while. Don't give in to despondency.

Saturday, 6th May
Moon trine Pluto

It seems that the entire universe is full of hidden meanings from your point of view today. A casual comment may be analysed in depth for any concealed message. You'll be on the lookout for omens, and it depends on your own frame of mind whether these signs and wonders will be good or bad. Try to take it a little easier, for if an emotional situation has got you that tense then it's time to take a step back from it for a while.

Sunday, 7th May
Moon trine Jupiter

With a good aspect between the Moon and Jupiter there should be a considerable easing in your emotional state. This is a day to breathe a sigh of relief, settle down into an aura of comfort and affection, and generally take it easy. Of course, you tend to be a stranger to quiet relaxation so involve yourself in an activity that you actually like. A daytrip in company with one you love is a very good idea.

Monday, 8th May
Moon conjunct Mars

Your entire chart is energized by the Moon's conjunction with your ruler Mars today. This should inspire and activate all the romantic potentials in your life. The trouble is that you could get a little big headed now, so you'll have to guard against being just a shade too forceful, especially with a lover. Don't be too impulsive and domineering and you won't spoil the splendid day.

Tuesday, 9th May
Moon square Jupiter

The excellent optimism created by yesterday's stars continues, yet your problem now is knowing when to quit while you're ahead. It might have done to push your luck recently but today caution should be your watchword. I know that your hopes have been lifted but you also have to keep your feet on the ground. In a work or health situation, listen to the words of a friend who has your welfare at heart.

Wednesday, 10th May
Moon opposite Saturn

You really mustn't expect everything to go just the way you want every day. The optimism could be seriously knocked now as the Moon opposes the sober planet Saturn. You'll be made very aware of all those circumstances that restrict your progress, and if you don't take care, you'll be plunged in a pit of gloom. Try to take a realistic look at the way things are going without giving in to depression and you'll arrive at a reasonable assessment of where you actually are. It's better than it looks.

Thursday, 11th May
Moon sextile Pluto

If there's been a health worry that's been nagging away at the back of your mind, then today's stars encourage you to find out exactly what the problem is. It'll probably turn out to be nothing at all, but think of the sense of relief when a doctor, dentist or nurse actually tells you that you're fighting fit.

Friday, 12th May
Mercury opposite Jupiter

Aries people are often aggressive in speech so opposition to your viewpoint is nothing new to you. Today however the opposition between Mercury and Jupiter shows that you aren't really prepared for the stubborn tenacity with which others hold to their opinions. You can't win an argument now, you'll only succeed in those around you digging in their heels, so try to avoid confrontation.

Saturday, 13th May
Venus square Neptune

There's an old saying that promises are cheap, the problem is that you'll be inclined to believe in them today. You don't need a glib con-man just now, because you're far too ready to con yourself. Again the message is keep your feet on the ground. Just because you want to believe something doesn't necessarily make it true. Take care, or you'll raise your hopes too high.

Sunday, 14th May
Moon opposite Sun

Today's Full Moon brings an intense emotional experience which you may find difficult to handle. Your feelings have been going through a roller coaster phase recently and this has had the effect of bringing psychological problems to the surface. Now you have to face your fears and admit to yourself that you're a little more vulnerable than you'd care to let on. It may be uncomfortable but this is a good influence, freeing you from hangovers of the past.

Monday, 15th May
Moon conjunct Pluto

For many it's the start of the Monday blues, but for you it's a powerful and amorous time. Your passions are enhanced by the conjunction of the Moon and Pluto, so sexual and intimate issues predominate in your thoughts. Inhibitions fade now and you are in a forceful and attractive frame of mind.

Tuesday, 16th May
Venus into Taurus

The entry of Venus into her own sign of Taurus will do your financial fortunes the world of good in the next couple of weeks. This is the start of a profitable time in which money will come in more easily than it has in the recent past. The true value of things too becomes an issue now and you'll realize that quality of life is equally as important as making cash. You'll desire tasteful surroundings and comfort while Venus remains in Taurus.

Wednesday, 17th May
Sun trine Neptune

The Sun's positive aspect to Neptune gives you the sense that financial security is not that far away. It's true that fortune smiles on your prospects of worldly wealth but it's important not to overstate your case or take too much for granted. Effort is still required to make the maximum profit so don't rest on your laurels just yet.

Thursday, 18th May
Sun square Mars

Keep that fiery Aries temper under control today. The Sun's harsh aspect to Mars makes it too easy to blow minor financial concerns out of all proportion. You may even think that you're being reasonable; unfortunately those around you will know that's not the case. Try to address worries sensibly rather than taking out your frustrations on those who would support you given half a chance.

Friday, 19th May
Moon sextile Pluto

Decisions made behind closed doors have got a profound influence at your place of work today. There's no need to fret: all this secrecy has got a good reason behind it. When you get the go ahead, you'll realize that anxiety was a waste of effort. No matter what the scenario you have to be patient. Your career progress will be helped along by this.

Saturday, 20th May
Sun opposite Pluto

Though the more general financial picture is good, it wouldn't do to ignore any troublesome details now. The Sun's opposition to Pluto urges caution. If investment, hire purchase or insurance matters are involved then take a good long look at the small print of contracts. Don't be tempted by get-rich-quick schemes, and don't commit yourself to spending more than you can afford.

Sunday, 21st May
Sun into Gemini

Any communication difficulties, or misunderstandings stand a good chance of being resolved as the Sun moves into the sign of Gemini today. It's time to pour oil on troubled waters and sort out any disagreements and hasty words that were spoken in the past. Your social life too is due for a welcome boost since you'll be in an extrovert mood. For the next month even the most casual conversation could point the way forward, so do remember to spend time listening as well as talking.

Monday, 22nd May
Moon square Mercury

I just knew all that talking was a mixed blessing. Your mind is racing so fast you can't help causing misunderstandings just now. You may also receive some wounding criticism, though you must admit that you're being a touch over sensitive. If these hurtful words were actually meant to be constructive then you could do worse than to think hard about the issues they raise.

Tuesday, 23rd May
Moon trine Pluto

The Moon's monthly round again makes a positive contact with Pluto today encouraging you to take a look at some of your internal motivations and desires. There's no doubt that you are getting to understand what makes you tick pretty well so you'll be more than ready to abandon old prejudices and rigid attitudes that have previously held you back.

Wednesday, 24th May
Mercury retrograde, Mars square Pluto

It's bound to be an intense and passionate day when Mars and Pluto cause an inner tension which will be expressed within a relationship. Mercury going retrograde doesn't help the scenario. Love and hate are just two of the extremes of emotion which you're prone to now. Perhaps you should consider a creative way of externalizing your feelings because you could be gripped by a romantic obsession which needs some positive expression.

Thursday, 25th May
Mars into Virgo

Your working life and daily habits come into sharp focus now as your ruling planet Mars enters the sign of Virgo. This shows an active and progressive period in which many of your past, non-productive ways of going about things fall by the wayside. Mars in Virgo is good news for your ambitions, and also for the state of your health: if you have been feeling poorly then you should now experience a renewed vitality.

Friday, 26th May
Moon into Taurus

As the Moon reaches Taurus it's time for you to sit back to reassess how far you've come, and what you've achieved materially speaking. As you look over your possessions it wouldn't be a bad thing to remember how and where you started. You aren't doing so badly after all.

Saturday, 27th May
Moon conjunct Venus

If you're feeling at all weak then don't venture anywhere near expensive shops because you're too prone to the impulse-buying syndrome today. Attractiveness is more important to you than value at the moment so the temptation to blow your cash on a luxury item is too strong for comfort. Hoard your resources now and leave shopping trips until you're less impetuous.

Sunday, 28th May
Moon opposite Pluto

This could be the long dark Sunday of the soul if you aren't careful. Boredom is the danger today and with you listless and frustrated it's going to be awful for anyone around you. Remember that the stars only incline you to a course of action, they don't compel it, so shake yourself out of this mood and do something positive. You aren't helping anyone, least of all yourself by giving in to a dull influence.

Monday, 29th May
Moon conjunct Sun

Today's New Moon brings good news, possibly concerning your family. It also enhances your social life, ushering in an active and enjoyable time. Those Ariens who are involved in educational affairs can now be confident that your academic progress is assured. Community matters too are boosted and you'll find yourself in the company of like-minded people for a while.

Tuesday, 30th May
Moon square Saturn

Even though the trends are working in your favour, you seem to have a nagging doubt as to whether all will go as well as expected. This could be something to do with a deeply seated lack of self-belief. If that's so then make the effort to shrug it off now. Just because worldly events aren't moving fast enough to suit you doesn't mean that there's anything wrong.

Wednesday, 31st May
Moon into Cancer

Though you've got the usual duties to perform, you'll be happiest in your own home, surrounded by your family today. With the Moon in her own sign of Cancer it's likely to be a nostalgic time in which you'll want to recall the good old days in the company of those who know you well. You need emotional security now.

June at a Glance

LOVE	♥	♥	♥		
WORK	★	★			
MONEY	$	$	$		
FITNESS	⊛	⊛	⊛		
LUCK	∪	∪	∪		

Thursday, 1st June
Sun opposite Jupiter

Though you are quite forward looking and confident today you may not receive the support you expect from relatives. In fact, you could feel somewhat let down by their negative attitudes to your aspirations and ideas. Don't let this apparent coldness deceive you for your relations have important concerns of their own and are preoccupied. Concentrate on inner strength, you've got plenty of that.

Friday, 2nd June
Moon trine Pluto

You like to keep up a tough, go ahead front but today's sensitive planets show you how sentimental you can be. You'll have an instinctive understanding of family members' feelings now so you should show them how much you sympathize with their troubles. Unfairly, Aries people have the reputation for being selfish, yet you do have a caring side. Don't be afraid to let this side show.

Saturday, 3rd June
Moon trine Jupiter

There's a twinkle in your eye today for the excellent aspect between the Moon and Jupiter enhances the romantic side of your nature. This is an adventurous influence favouring journeys in company with someone you love. If passion holds little appeal then you should turn the good vibes to more creative projects because your talents shine now.

Sunday, 4th June
Moon square Venus

Comfort and pleasure are the watchwords today. Serious concerns leave you cold as you take your pick from a variety of happy activities. Love and romance are highlights now, but you also need the company of friends to make the day complete. This is a chance to cast away stress and simply enjoy yourself.

Monday, 5th June
Venus sextile Saturn

The working week begins with a splendid opportunity to show how sensible and shrewd you can be. You're business minded now and have the chance to make some considerable profit simply because you see an opening where others only see a blank wall. The aspect between

Venus and Saturn is a very caring one though, so you're likely to spend your profits on someone else as soon as they've arrived.

Tuesday, 6th June
Sun conjunct Mercury

There's no doubt that your mental powers are on top form today. The conjunction of the Sun and Mercury lets your intelligence shine. You are particularly persuasive now too, so it shouldn't be difficult to win even the most stubborn and entrenched person over to your cause.

Wednesday, 7th June
Venus trine Neptune

There's an atmosphere of selfless caring about you today. The splendid link between Venus and Neptune shows that you're about to benefit from a favour from someone in authority. It just goes to show how well you are thought of by those who matter professionally. You'll also be inclined to share your good fortune, which shows that you're a considerate soul too.

Thursday, 8th June
Moon trine Mercury

If you're the type that keeps your thoughts to yourself, then spare a thought for your partner who could be wondering what's going on in that brain of yours. Today's stars give you the chance to tell all and explain your motivations and desires. Don't be afraid of rejection or laughter because you'll find that someone special is very much in tune with your thoughts.

Friday, 9th June
Venus opposite Pluto

With a trying aspect between Pluto and Venus this is a day

for passions to run high. The sexual magnetism is strong but so are underlying stresses. You'll experience them all today, but at least this will be a golden opportunity for you and your partner to clear the air and resolve past frustrations.

Saturday, 10th June
Venus into Gemini

Venus enters the sign of Gemini today heralding a time of social fun and new romantic encounters. For the next couple of weeks women particularly will have a profound influence over your ideas. This planetary movement also adds a flirtatious aspect to your character and shows a splendid time for travel, meeting new friends and showing yourself off at your best.

Sunday, 11th June
Moon sextile Uranus

It's a highly original and inventive day. The Moon aspects Uranus and fires inspiration directly into your brain. Problems that you once thought insoluble yield to your perception now. When you consider career affairs for instance, your next steps should be obvious, though you should bear in mind that it wouldn't be wise to tell everyone of your upcoming plans.

Monday, 12th June
Moon conjunct Jupiter

Though there might be a test of your self-belief at some point today it's important that you cling to your faith. The Moon conjuncts Jupiter now and lifts your mind out of a rut while setting your sights on affairs in distant parts of the world. You can't be bothered with petty worries and small-minded attitudes. You've got bigger, better concepts to dwell on.

Tuesday, 13th June
Moon opposite Sun

The focus of the heavens concentrates on your intellect at this Full Moon. You'll have had some inkling of what can be achieved and you'll now be ready to look at your options. It may be that a trip abroad is planned now, and that would be a good thing because you'll get the chance to add to your experience of life. Foreign cultures and other philosophies will be a stimulus to your mind. The Full Moon favours matters of faith and educational pursuits.

Wednesday, 14th June
Mars square Jupiter

It's obvious that you've had your sights lifted out of a rut but that's no reason to let your new-found insight go to your head. The world seems a marvellous place just now, but don't be fooled into thinking that universal harmony will just happen of its own accord. Keep your feet on the ground. Be optimistic by all means, but going over the top about it isn't doing anyone any favours.

Thursday, 15th June
Moon conjunct Uranus

It's a day for your professional life to be shaken up in a most alarming way. But let the shock waves pass and you'll find that you're in a better position. Keep your mind on where you want to go and what you want to achieve. Don't allow petty office politics to intrude and you're on an innovative path to success.

Friday, 16th June
Sun square Saturn

Though you are clear about your own mind and what you want to accomplish, you can't seem to explain your position or make any progress today. Talking at cross purposes, unexplained prejudice and downright stubbornness are a few of the obstacles you'll meet with now. Try to be patient, and hold onto your common sense because that's the only thing you can rely on now.

Saturday, 17th June
Mercury direct

A lot of tension is dissipated as Mercury resumes direct motion today. This is a good chance to sort out misunderstandings, untangle confused thinking and get more mobile. Short trips which lead to happy meetings are the favoured activity this Saturday.

Sunday, 18th June
Venus opposite Jupiter

It's too easy to tempt you with forbidden delights this Sunday. Jupiter and Venus are playing on your weaknesses now and you're not only likely to give in, but to embrace your failings. Diets, and resolutions such as giving up smoking are set to suffer from your weak-willed attitude. But, then again it is said that a little of what you fancy does you good. Just don't go over the top.

Monday, 19th June
Moon square Sun

You're quite introverted this Monday. There's no doubt that you're thinking deep thoughts and getting intrigued by the most obscure facts and subjects. Don't let this pleasurable reverie distract you from the outer world though, because there's a meeting due with someone who's likely to become very special indeed.

Tuesday, 20th June
Moon sextile Uranus

The Aries brain is working overtime today. Your imagination

is so original and inventive that ideas are leaping unbidden to the forefront of your mind. If you're clever you'll jot some of these down because inspiration doesn't always strike and it'd be good to hang on to a few of the ones that occur now.

Wednesday, 21st June
Sun into Cancer

It's Midsummer as the Sun moves into your fellow cardinal sign of Cancer. This time of year makes you quite nostalgic, so it might be an idea to gather friends and family around you now. This is a good period for sorting out any domestic squabbles and generally setting your house in order. The coming month has a distinctly homey feel to it so it's pretty certain that you'll be happiest in your own surroundings.

Thursday, 22nd June
Venus square Mars

The demands of your working world will be heavy today, and you may feel the effects of stress, possibly in the form of headaches or backache. The harsh aspect between Venus and Mars shows how far you've got to go to make your ideas a reality. This is not a signal to be downhearted, however: look after your own well-being today and you'll soon be back in fighting form.

Friday, 23rd June
Moon trine Mars

It's no wonder that Aries people are reminiscent of a battering ram. When there's an obstacle before you, you won't rest until you have broken it down. Friday's stars show you to be something of a workaholic, and I must admit your capacity for hard graft is impressive. Though I applaud your efforts, however, make sure you don't wear yourself out.

Saturday, 24th June
Moon trine Uranus

Impulse rules the day as far as Aries people are concerned. This is not a time for passively working out your next moves, it's time to get going. If you've decided on an ambitious financial move then follow your instincts. If you thought about it sensibly, you might come to the conclusion that a purchase was beyond your means. On the other hand, if you do lay out the cash, you aren't going to regret it.

Sunday, 25th June
Moon opposite Jupiter

It's a very restless Sunday as the Moon opposes Jupiter. You're likely to feel bored and stifled by the familiar now and yearn for a little adventure. Travel may be fraught with delays though so it may be wisest to confine yourself to expanding your knowledge via reading rather than risking a traffic jam.

Monday, 26th June
Moon conjunct Mercury

You might think that you speak in a reasoned, clear voice today, but your emotional intensity is showing through. You've obviously got a lot of conviction now and you can't fail to be persuasive and eloquent when you display such sincerity. If a close partnership has been going through a sticky patch then it's time you expressed your true feelings.

Tuesday, 27th June
Saturn sextile Neptune

Those in your working environment may think that you're off on a flight of fancy, but it just goes to show how wrong people can be. As Saturn positively aspects Neptune, all your dreams and inspirations are firmly grounded in reality. It's up to you to make them come true, but it is within your power. Have faith in yourself and don't allow the negative views of others to affect your view of your direction.

Wednesday, 28th June
Moon conjunct Sun

The New Moon in Cancer puts extra emphasis on your home life. Many Ariens will be considering moving to a new area, but if nothing so ambitious is planned, it's still a good time to make some much needed changes to your environment. For some, this will take the form of DIY. For others it could be as simple as sorting out some new house rules that everyone should abide by.

Thursday, 29th June
Moon opposite Uranus

There's a rebellious astral influence today, for the Moon is in opposition to Uranus and that means that you won't take kindly to being tied down, even to a promise that you've previously made. You can't see why you should obey rules or indeed authority in any form. Cool down Aries, or you could end up in hot water.

Friday, 30th June
Moon trine Jupiter

The last day of June and it's time to think ahead. Your personal life is in need of some attention as indeed is your own self-satisfaction in what you do. You need to display a creative and innovative side now. A holiday would be just the ticket. If you're attached then this could renew your relationship. If not, a meeting while away would fit the bill.

July at a Glance

LOVE	♥				
WORK	★	★	★	★	
MONEY	$	$	$		
FITNESS	(Ⓜ)				
LUCK	♘	♘			

Saturday, 1st July
Venus square Saturn

A host of minor worries are revealed by today's square aspect between Venus and Saturn. It's important not to over-react when you feel that communication with a lover is too cool for comfort. Before you jump to any conclusions you should play the waiting game and see what this evening brings.

Sunday, 2nd July
Moon square Pluto

'Curiosity killed the cat,' they say, but the consequences of your subtle enquiries aren't as serious as that. That's not to say that you won't be disturbed by a financial revelation today. It may be that you are being too hasty in your assessment of dishonest dealings. I know patience doesn't sit easily with you so voice your suspicions. It's the only way you'll get any peace.

Monday, 3rd July
Mercury square Mars

Being a person with a fiery nature it's sometimes too easy to express the full force of your personality without realizing how aggressive you actually seem. Verbal aggression is the problem today and you could offend the sensibilities of someone you wouldn't hurt for the world. If in doubt, hold your tongue.

Tuesday, 4th July
Moon square Venus

Tuesday looks like a lethargic day for usually active Aries people. It's obvious that you've bitten off far more than you can chew in a work situation and are now suffering the after effects. You won't want to be bothered with anything strenuous today.

Wednesday, 5th July
Venus into Cancer

As Venus enters Cancer you have another heaven-sent chance to pour oil on any troubled family waters. It may be that you have to take a back seat when a female relative makes it quite clear that she rules the roost. Tasteful decoration too is a focus of attention and you may feel that your home could do with a lick of paint.

Thursday, 6th July
Moon square Uranus

You may start out quite calmly but work colleagues are jumpy and nervous today. It's obvious that something has set the cat amongst the pigeons and you won't know what it is. If you don't keep up your common sense you'll panic like the rest by the end of the day. You'd do well to find out what's going on.

Friday, 7th July
Mercury square Saturn

Yesterday's troublesome astrological scene shows no sign of ebbing quite yet and you'll be caught up in complications, rumours and anxieties. If you were to stop to think for a while you'd soon work out that there's very little to worry you. Take a deep breath Aries and look past the obvious panic of your workmates.

Saturday, 8th July
Moon sextile Mars

The weekend break has occurred at just the right time psychologically speaking, since you were finding work pressures quite trying. Now you can look at things from a distance it's easy to see what's been going on. There's very little that could get past your shrewd gaze today.

Sunday, 9th July
Moon sextile Uranus

Even though it's a day of rest, your mind will be ticking over with all the implications of a major change at work. You will have worked out by now that this could be to your advantage if you play your cards right. Sorting out a strategy is the favoured mental activity today.

Monday, 10th July
Mercury into Cancer

The past exerts a powerful influence as Mercury enters your fellow cardinal sign of the Crab. You'll find that things long forgotten will somehow re-enter your life over the next couple of weeks. An interest in your family heritage may develop, or possibly a new-found passion for antiques. Some good, meaningful conversations in the family will prove enlightening.

Tuesday, 11th July
Mars trine Neptune

You'll have to use some cunning to get your own way today. The usual Aries approach of 'head down and charge' isn't going to work. You'll have to restrain your impatience and fish a little for information. You should follow any clue that will lead to career progress but don't reveal your hand.

Wednesday, 12th July
Moon opposite Sun

The Full Moon today shines onto your career and direction in life. You know that some changes are inevitable so you should look at the ways in which you can adapt to prevailing conditions. Old, outworn thinking will have to go now so be prepared for new career suggestions. You may also be quite sensitive to any hint of criticism now.

Thursday, 13th July
Moon conjunct Uranus

There's no use sticking to the tried and true when the Moon conjuncts Uranus. The more unconventional the thinking the more likely it is to succeed. You're in an innovative mood, ready for anything, and should be quite capable of providing a few surprises of your own.

Friday, 14th July
Moon into Aquarius

The original and innovative influence of Uranus continues today when the Moon transits Aquarius. You'll be stimulated by new ideas and will be anxious to meet with people who have a positive and possibly eccentric view of life.

Saturday, 15th July
Moon square Pluto

You should resist all temptations to part with your cash

today. Any attempt to stretch the budget will give you cause for regret. You're easily swayed in opinion now so a well-meaning but misguided friend could easily lead you astray. Try to be strong and know when to say NO!

Sunday, 16th July
Moon trine Venus

The finer things of life have a delightful appeal today. You're in a cultured frame of mind susceptible to refined music and fine art. There's also a romantic side to this Venusian influence, so it's a time to indulge yourself in pleasure.

Monday, 17th July
Sun opposite Neptune

The Sun opposes Neptune this Monday which doesn't do anything for your self-confidence. You're likely to be prone to vague fears and anxieties now. If you were more logical you'd see that there's very little to be concerned about as long as you aren't gullible. Avoid glib talkers like the plague.

Tuesday, 18th July
Sun trine Saturn

In total contrast to yesterday's confusions, the Sun's aspect to Saturn puts everything in perspective. In fact, you'll be anxious to put every area of your life in order now. The home is the main scene of your reforming zeal. 'A place for everything, and everything in its place' is your motto for this practical day.

Wednesday, 19th July
Mars trine Uranus

This is a day when the true force and drive of the Aries personality shines through. The strong aspect between Mars and Uranus ensures that in all work and professional matters you'll get your own way and show yourself off to the best advantage. You can show such qualities of leadership now that no one's in any doubt that you are a formidable contender.

Thursday, 20th July
Moon into Taurus

Financial planning is the order of the day as the Moon transits the sign of Taurus. You may find it boring but some thought given to your monetary position will pay dividends in the future. Be as sensible as you possibly can.

Friday, 21st July
Mars into Libra

Mars enters your solar house of partnerships today, which in your case is the diplomatic sign of Libra. As you can imagine, forceful, dynamic Mars doesn't quite fit into such a gentle sign so until 7th September you'll have to take care that you don't stomp on the sensibilities of your partner. Try to be more thoughtful and confine your aggression for business.

Saturday, 22nd July
Sun opposite Uranus

This could be a day full of irritation and impatience. The Sun opposes Uranus now so you'll have to resist the temptation to take out your frustrations on your family. You may get more than you expect if you go around snapping irritably. The worm may turn and a confrontation just now isn't a thing to be encouraged.

Sunday, 23rd July
Sun into Leo

A lot of your frustration fades today as the Sun makes his entry into your fellow fire sign of Leo. This movement highlights your creative potential and self-expression. You'll feel more free and able to show the world your talent. You'll attract admirers by the score over the next month because this area of your chart also governs romance.

Monday, 24th July
Venus opposite Neptune

Diplomacy isn't a concept that often occurs to most Ariens, yet that's what's required today. You need kid gloves to handle colleagues and family members who are troubled. At least you will understand why they're in this state, but will you be able to tread carefully enough? Avoid any tendency to indulge in escapist fantasies now. It's not a time to make far-reaching decisions.

Tuesday, 25th July
Mercury into Leo

A fun-filled, playful time is heralded as Mercury enters Leo today. Creativity and artistic accomplishment fill your life as you express your talents with consummate ease. You have until 10th August to communicate honestly with your lover. Children too may bring out a child-like and innocent side of yourself.

Wednesday, 26th July
Sun sextile Mars

This is a good day for pleasure and romance. The playful atmosphere of the last few days continues as the Sun aspects your ruler Mars. Now you also have great vitality and enthusiasm for life. You may feel you want to make a casual emotional link into something more permanent. You could sweep a lover off his or her feet.

Thursday, 27th July
Moon conjunct Sun

The New Moon in Leo gives a boost to all creation. News of pregnancies, births and the expression of talent is to be expected over the next couple of weeks. You'll feel the need to express a long-dormant side to your character. Don't delay because as soon as you gain the courage to stand out from the crowd and do what you want the happier you'll be.

Friday, 28th July
Sun conjunct Mercury

If ever there was a day for an amorous heart to heart, this is it. The Sun unites with Mercury making intimate conversation and declarations of love so much easier. Don't waste this tender opportunity to express your love. You'll be a witty and amusing companion this Friday.

Saturday, 29th July
Venus into Leo

As if you weren't in a romantic mood already, Venus gets in on the act today making it more certain that you're about to be swept wholeheartedly up in an amorous dream. If Mr or Miss Right hasn't turned up yet, don't despair because in true matchmaking style, Venus will soon put that situation to rights.

Sunday, 30th July
Mars sextile Jupiter

Happiness, optimism and adventure are the features of the day as Mars and Jupiter cast a marvellous aura over your chart. Seek out new experience, get out and about with your partner and open your eyes to the myriad possibilities that await you. Unattached Aries people may find that situation changes.

Monday, 31st July
Moon trine Uranus

You may feel somewhat listless and misunderstood today but a colleague stands by to provide a few words of kindness. You'll be impressed by the compassion of someone you may know only slightly. This could be the start of a fulfilling friendship. If you can, help them in some way.

August at a Glance

LOVE	♥	♥	♥	♥	♥
WORK	★	★	★	★	
MONEY	$	$	$	$	$
FITNESS	◉	◉	◉	◉	◉
LUCK	♘	♘	♘	♘	

Tuesday, 1st August
Moon conjunct Mars

There's no point in waiting around for anyone else when the Moon conjuncts Mars. You'll have to chart your own course now with the full confidence that you've got the dynamism and enthusiasm to make a success of whatever you do. Aries people are said to be independent and this is your chance to show it.

Wednesday, 2nd August
Jupiter direct

A lot of your convictions have gone through a profound alteration since Jupiter went retrograde in May. Today, the giant planet resumes its direct course and you can take stock of the changes of opinion you've experienced. A lot of confusions will now be resolved. You may feel that your luck improves as your mind clears.

Thursday, 3rd August
Venus trine Jupiter

The fortunate influence of Jupiter combines with Venus now making this a day to remember. Love, happiness, luck and optimism are the gifts of these two most beneficial planets. Links with someone of a different national or ethnic background could develop in a romantic way. Children too could encourage you to look at the world in a positive way. This is a deeply fulfilling time.

Friday, 4th August
Moon square Sun

Though you're still in the mood for fun and adventure, those close to home don't appreciate your apparently selfish actions. A money worry may emerge today, which will do nothing to encourage any harmony. Very little can be resolved today so wait until this stellar influence passes.

Saturday, 5th August
Moon sextile Uranus

Prepare to be surprised and even stunned by revelations made today. I hope you've got nothing to hide because no piece of information, no matter how private, is safe now. At least it's a way of laying cards on the table, and the long-term consequences of this are likely to be good.

Sunday, 6th August
Moon trine Mercury

It's a good day to share your knowledge and experience with someone younger who is in need of some advice. The Moon's aspect to Mercury makes you the perfect person to guide a child in the right path now. The most serious situation can be viewed with humour and that always helps to take the sting out of hard facts.

Monday, 7th August
Venus sextile Mars

The week begins on a highly emotional note. With the combination of Venus and Mars, both in houses that relate to partnerships and romance, affairs of the heart are the primary concern now. It's said that the path of true love never runs smooth, but today the amorous route is calm and full of affection.

Tuesday, 8th August
Pluto direct

Pluto resumes direct motion today setting a long-term influence into effect. This could be your last chance to transform your private affairs. This could relate to shared finances, insurance and investments, but it's more likely to bring to light sexual issues which may be troubling. By November, Pluto will have entered another area of the chart so think deeply now.

Wednesday, 9th August
Mercury square Pluto

It's a fact of life that some subjects are difficult to think about, let alone discuss, but today you must be brave and talk over deeply disturbing issues that have been plaguing you. It's a time for honesty and possibly confession. It may be hard, but you'll feel better for expressing your inner self.

Thursday, 10th August
Mercury into Virgo

As Mercury speeds into his own sign of Virgo, Aries people will feel the call of duty very strongly. That doesn't only apply to you of course. You won't be able to bear inefficiency or sloppy work around you now because a perfectionist tendency makes itself felt in your character. I dare say that a few sharp words will be spoken in keeping with Mercury's critical nature in this sign.

Friday, 11th August
Moon square Pluto

It's not wise to take too much on face value today. A smiling face may conceal a betrayal of trust and confidence. Honeyed words are to be treated with suspicion. Don't let anyone pull the wool over your eyes by involving you in affairs that aren't quite above board.

Saturday, 12th August
Moon square Jupiter

You're delving into your own private world again today. The power of your imagination is very strong and you can see things not as they are, but as they should be in an ideal world. You may review your life and realize how much you have learned as well as how much you've gained in the material sense.

Sunday, 13th August
Mercury square Jupiter

Just because you want a quiet time this Sunday it isn't wise to fob others off with easy promises that you've got no intention of keeping. This isn't the way to keep friends or even any credibility. Of course you may think that your words will be fulfilled, but events out of your control decree otherwise. Keep your lip zipped.

Monday, 14th August
Moon trine Venus

The love life receives a welcome boost today as the Moon and Venus conspire to lift the passionate intensity. Being a creature of impulse it shouldn't be too much of a problem to arrange an evening of amorous dalliance. A trip to the theatre or cinema would bring a little sparkle into your relationship.

Tuesday, 15th August
Moon square Uranus

It's not a day for the Aries temper to flare, or indeed for any over reaction since people in authority are a little volatile themselves. Keep the peace at all costs now, for an explosion from you could set off a chain reaction with unpredictable consequences.

Wednesday, 16th August
Moon trine Mercury

It's a good day for making solid progress on the career front. You can project an image of someone who gets things done. Your efforts will find favour with those who are important now. Those Ariens who are out of a job may find that an opportunity occurring today will solve your problems.

Thursday, 17th August
Saturn sextile Neptune

Though it may seem that your head is full of outrageous fantasies and idealistic concepts, there is method in the way you're thinking now. Saturn has returned to its sextile aspect with Neptune and in so doing gives a firm, steady base of assumptions on which to base your ideas. Don't allow others to knock your faith in your own future.

Friday, 18th August
Moon trine Uranus

Today provides a test for Aries people. You aren't generally the world's natural savers so when an opportunity occurs for you to get an excellent long-term return for an outlay of cash, you'll have to think long and hard about it. Put your money somewhere safe, where it can work for you. You'll only spend the lot otherwise.

Saturday, 19th August
Moon opposite Jupiter

The most casual conversation will be fraught with misunderstanding today. If it stops there, then all's well and good but if serious issues are discussed then you'll leave others with totally the wrong impression. Keep everything light now and don't be drawn into committing yourself to schemes you are unsure of.

Sunday, 20th August
Sun conjunct Venus

This could turn out to be one of the most glamorous days of the year. The Sun meets up with Venus in your house of leisure and romance, casting a brilliant glow over your love life and refined good taste. You are likely to be inspired by the presence of someone you love and could turn this influence into an artistic creation of lasting beauty.

Monday, 21st August
Sun square Pluto

Your emotional states are very strong at the moment, but the Sun's harsh aspect to Pluto shows that this passion has a down side. Obsession and a smothering affection are likely to be turn offs today, so try to hold back on an overwhelming expression of desire.

Tuesday, 22nd August
Moon square Mars

It's a pity that your temper's got a short fuse because someone very special could be on the receiving end of your wrath through no fault of their own today. I know your mood is due to stress but you can't always expect others to be so understanding. Cool it Aries.

Wednesday, 23rd August
Sun into Virgo

The Sun moves into your house of health, duty and habits today bringing in a month when all these issues must be addressed. There'll be no better time to get rid of some practices, such as smoking, that aren't doing your physical well-being any good. If you are in doubt then sort out your worries with some medical advice. In work affairs, you'll be efficient and resourceful.

Thursday, 24th August
Mercury opposite Saturn

It seems you have a mental block today. No matter how hard you try you can't get to grips with a problem. The trouble is that Mercury's opposition to Saturn has clouded your thinking processes. The solution might be right under your nose but you can't see it. Have some patience, the clouds will clear.

Friday, 25th August
Mercury trine Neptune

It's time to stop thinking about your own immediate interests and repay a favour or kindness that has been done for you in the past. Show yourself to be a thoughtful and generous person, your reputation can only increase by a unselfish action now.

Saturday, 26th August
Moon conjunct Sun

Today's New Moon puts the spotlight on the state of your health. If you're to achieve all the goals that you've set yourself then you must realize that your body's got to be up to the task as well as your mind. Think about your bad habits, because there's no better time to start a diet or exercise programme.

Sunday, 27th August
Moon opposite Saturn

You may feel a little under the weather today. The Moon's opposition to Saturn casts an aura of gloom over you. It's probably work pressure that's at the root of your mood and you desperately need some light relief. Keep away from arduous tasks now. Be easy on yourself or your health may suffer.

Monday, 28th August
Venus square Jupiter

Stress is causing some disruption to your routine at the moment. If you're prone to stomach upsets or heartburn leave alcohol and spicy foods to another day. It's time to be good to your body, because if you are, your body will be good to you.

Tuesday, 29th August
Mercury into Libra

I know that your working life has been a source of strain recently but that has caused you to look inward and neglect your partner. Mercury has now entered your house of relationships so now's the time to set emotional affairs in order. Tell your spouse what's on your mind and you'll meet an affectionate display of sympathy and understanding.

Wednesday, 30th August
Sun square Jupiter

A disruption to your working day may turn out to be a blessing in disguise since it gets you out of a familiar, if oppressive environment for at least a while. Take plenty of breaks today, because you psychologically need to see a few new faces.

Thursday, 31st August
Mars sextile Jupiter

Partners of all kinds, whether emotionally linked or business colleagues will encourage you to broaden your personal horizons now. Your ruler Mars is in splendid aspect with Jupiter and those around you will want you to fulfil your potential. You may be forced to stand out from the crowd and take a new, adventurous direction. There's nothing to fear in this, so aim high.

September at a Glance

LOVE	♥	♥			
WORK	★	★			
MONEY	$	$	$	$	
FITNESS	〰	〰	〰	〰	
LUCK	♘				

Friday, 1st September
Moon conjunct Pluto

The Aries sex appeal hits boiling point today, so you'll need an outlet for all that passion. You'll have a strong desire to let a special person know the depth of your feelings. You are irresistibly attractive now.

Saturday, 2nd September
Mars square Uranus

Other people's opinions will get short shrift from you as the fiery aspect between Mars and Uranus puts you into a rebellious and stubborn mood for much of the day. You are intolerant of opposition in any form, and will be quite prepared to dismiss contrary views as idiotic. You need to burn off some excess energy constructively.

Sunday, 3rd September
Mercury sextile Jupiter

It just goes to show that you aren't all bad. It's fortunate that after some irritable outburst, there is someone who understands and still believes in you. It's obvious that you are an important pillar in some else's life so respond with some affection now.

Monday, 4th September
Moon trine Venus

Your eyes are set on the professional stars and you aren't the only one who's sure that they are attainable. Your partner, friends and colleagues have full confidence in you, and will be all too willing to assist in any small way to your eventual success.

Tuesday, 5th September
Moon square Mars

Impatience is an Aries trait that get things done, but quite often gets you into hot water. It's important that you don't leap before you look today or you could set off a quarrel that'd be difficult to control. Keep a cool head Aries and don't over-react.

Wednesday, 6th September
Moon trine Mercury

This is an excellent day for making plans with your partner in life. Your hopes are enhanced and in tune. Talk things over now and see how much of a vision you share. Your friends too offer plenty of encouragement for your ideals.

Thursday, 7th September
Mars into Scorpio

Your ruling planet, Mars enters his other sign of Scorpio today and warns you to keep a close eye on the finances. Some of your joint plans may be expensive so it's important not to blow more than you can afford. Sexually, you'll be a dynamo. You may meet a guru, or at least someone who has a profound influence on the way you think. This should be an enlightening time.

Friday, 8th September
Moon trine Mars

The energy levels are quite low this Sunday, and though you've got plenty of plans, you may not feel inclined to start just yet. Try to make the effort to work your way through all of your tasks one at a time. Your partner too needs some attention so a romantic gesture would go down well.

Saturday, 9th September
Moon opposite Sun

It's important to be as clear as day as this Full Moon casts a cloud of illusion over much of what you do. Women around you are especially deceptive, whether they mean to be or not. You'll be inclined to drown your sorrows but indulging in escapism isn't going to solve anything.

Sunday, 10th September
Venus trine Neptune

The dreamy influence continues as Venus makes a positive aspect to Neptune encouraging you to allow your imagination free rein. You may find work pressures too difficult to bear without the odd day dream. This is an excellent aspect for all those involved with creative work because your talents will shine. However, money matters should be left well alone.

Monday, 11th September
Moon opposite Mercury

Be careful of what you say now, since your tongue wags so readily that you could let an important secret slip. A private revelation between you and your spouse will do more good than otherwise, but don't air personal affairs in public.

Tuesday, 12th September
Moon square Uranus

There's likely to be a personality clash between yourself and an authority figure today, unless of course you decide to keep a low profile. I know you don't agree with the official line but there's not much point in making an issue of it just now.

Wednesday, 13th September
Venus trine Uranus

You're full of inventive and creative ideas today, but the usual routine leaves you completely cold. A small break will work wonders if you can get about to meet interesting and unconventional people. You feel the call of the new and could do with a change from the old familiar faces. Today should be full of surprises.

Thursday, 14th September
Moon trine Venus

It's obvious that you're expressing a charming side to your personality at the moment, since all those around you are falling over themselves to get in your good books. The affection and goodwill expressed to you now are staggering.

Friday, 15th September
Venus sextile Pluto

If you feel dismayed by the cool attitude of an object of desire, then be prepared for a pleasant surprise. It's true that faint heart never won fair lady (or gentleman), so speak up, because you have the allure to win through all romantic obstacles now.

Saturday, 16th September
Venus into Libra

Close relationships are highlighted as Venus moves into her own sign of Libra. This is the start of a time of affectionate gestures, thoughtfulness and love. Affairs of the heart will go well at least until the end of October. If you're unattached, the next couple of weeks could see a change in your single state.

Sunday, 17th September
Moon square Venus

A quiet, undemanding Sunday is just what you need. Home comforts and the satisfaction of being surrounded by love show you that life really is worth living. Take this time to relax and build yourself up for the week ahead.

Monday, 18th September
Moon trine Mars

Fighting fit, and ready for action you'll be ready to take on the world and win this Monday. If you've got to promote yourself or your ideas, there won't be a better time to convince those who matter of your competence.

Tuesday, 19th September
Moon trine Pluto

If you examine your memories of the past you'll find that they bear more than a passing resemblance to your situation now. Family history and your childhood are issues once more. Don't shy away from even painful remembrance because you have the chance to gain a greater understanding of your life.

Wednesday, 20th September
Sun trine Uranus

Your working world is set to be transformed by the marvels of computer science and modern technology. I know you, you're a sucker for novelty and any gadget will take your fancy now. You're open to new innovations and novel ideas. Your professional life could take on a positive direction.

Thursday, 21st September
Moon sextile Mercury

It's time for fun and togetherness as the Moon and Mercury highlight romantic potentials and partnerships. Forget mundane worries and get out with the sole aim of enjoying yourself. The presence of someone special makes this a time to remember.

Friday, 22nd September
Mercury retrograde

Everything comes to a dead stop in your working environment as Mercury again pauses in his course. News of opportunities may now be delayed. Letters, phone calls and professional contacts are either mistimed or full of evasion. Don't worry, this period will pass, but you'll have to put up with it until 14th October.

Saturday, 23rd September
Sun into Libra

Emotional contentment and a renewed pleasure in your relationships is your lot as the Sun moves into your opposite sign of Libra today. You've got a lot of charm now, so the more sensitive side of your nature becomes more apparent. Affairs of the heart are enhanced for the next month.

Sunday, 24th September
Moon conjunct Sun

Close relationships are again the centre of your being as the New Moon in Libra promises a new start in amorous affairs. Those Aries folk who are married will find a renewed closeness to your other half, while rams who are single may find love in unexpected places.

Monday, 25th September
Moon sextile Jupiter

Today is the Jewish New Year, and what better way to celebrate the fact than by allowing the influence of Jupiter to stimulate the more idealistic and philosophical side of your nature. Travel is well starred now, as are all contacts with foreign people and ideas.

Tuesday, 26th September
Moon square Uranus

Surprises galore as Uranus inspires your partner to act in an odd manner. You never thought that he or she had such drive and originality. Be tolerant of apparent changes in your relationship; some of them will come to nothing. Others will tend to enhance rather than detract from your closeness.

Wednesday, 27th September
Moon conjunct Mars

Restraint is the key to personal success as the Moon conjuncts Mars in one of the most intimate areas of your chart. You may be tempted to use sexual allure to get your own way, or you may find yourself the victim of emotional blackmail. An authority figure could get above himself or you'll find that partnership funds are seriously depleted. Keep a sense of perspective.

Thursday, 28th September
Moon conjunct Pluto

Yesterday's theme continues, but this time on a more controlled note. The underlying problems may still be there but at least it's easier to cope with them now. You may see a way to fulfil longings that, as yet, haven't seen the light of day. This is a hopeful direction for the future.

Friday, 29th September
Moon conjunct Jupiter

This is really a day for optimism and happiness as the Moon contacts Jupiter. All your hopes are given a lift by this harmonious combination. Of course you are now in a lucky period, but don't rely on it too much. You've got to put some effort into your life as well as fate.

Saturday, 30th September
Moon square Saturn

After your optimistic hopes, the reaction sets in today and you feel let down with a bump. You can see the obstacles in front of you too clearly now but this is still not a reason for despondency. So there are some hurdles, you always knew that. Keep up the belief in yourself.

October at a Glance

LOVE	♥	♥	♥	♥	♥
WORK	★				
MONEY	$	$	$	$	$
FITNESS	◖				
LUCK	∪	∪			

Sunday, 1st October
Moon into Capricorn

October begins with the sense that you have to put forward an image of probity and respectability. You think that the impression you give is the most important thing at the moment, yet no matter what front you put up, you real qualities shine through.

Monday, 2nd October
Moon sextile Saturn

The call of duty is very strong when the Moon positively aspects Saturn. You're aware of the mountain of tasks that await you this week, yet if you take it slowly, methodically and sensibly there's no reason why your efforts shouldn't be crowned with success.

Tuesday, 3rd October
Moon sextile Pluto

For someone who's supposed to be tough, you have a sensitive side that you don't like admitting to. A few harsh words from a stressed out person hit you hard today. Try to understand the strain in the other person's life and not aggressively rise to the bait. You need some tolerance today.

Wednesday, 4th October
Venus square Neptune

You're a little too self-serving for comfort today. You'll be happy to weave a web of deceit hoping that an unflattering truth won't come to light. You're only deceiving yourself, and it would be better if you just admitted your fault immediately rather than risking the consequences when it gets out later.

Thursday, 5th October
Neptune direct

As the distant planet Neptune resumes its slow, direct course, you'll be reassured that your professional dreams have got some chance of fulfilment. You've got a long way to go yet, but you are on the right road. Trust your instincts.

Friday, 6th October
Uranus direct

Following in Neptune's footsteps, Uranus too heads back in the right direction promising a rapid change in your worldly status. This is all to the good as long as you're prepared to take on the challenges of new technology and new ways of thinking. If you've been stuck in a rut, there are signs that you'll soon be free for better things.

Saturday, 7th October
Venus square Uranus

It's obvious that things aren't happening fast enough to suit your impetuous nature. Psychologically you need a change, and if you can't find that in professional life just yet, you'll need some novelty on the social scene. New encounters are necessary, and may even lead to romance.

Sunday, 8th October
Moon opposite Sun

All close personal affairs need some scrutiny now. The Lunar Eclipse casts a shadow on your expectations in a relationship. Changes are inevitable, perhaps only surface ones, but any differences must come out into the open now if you want a healthy partnership in the future.

Monday, 9th October
Moon opposite Venus

Someone very close to you is feeling a terrible burden of insecurity now. It may be that some harsh facts recently faced have shaken confidence. Some reassurance from you is vital. Remember that you too can be prone to over-sensitivity so have some sympathy with one who needs your presence now.

Tuesday, 10th October
Venus into Scorpio

If you are considering charting your own independent course then Venus's entry into Scorpio warns you that this wouldn't be wise just now. A partner has need of you, at least to explain what you're about, and if you don't include him, or her, the hangover of this incident will be with you for a long time to come.

Wednesday, 11th October
Moon opposite Mars

Financial worries govern the day as the Moon opposes Mars in fiscal areas of your chart. Try not to over-react to any minor economic problems. Your temper is frayed but if you are systematic you can sort out monetary problems before they arise.

Thursday, 12th October
Moon opposite Pluto

Money matters again loom large, but they take on a more official nature today. The Moon's opposition to Pluto shows that tax, investment or alimony worries need to be dealt with now. Obstinacy won't solve anything, so you'll have to be prepared to give a little to gain a little.

Friday, 13th October
Moon trine Sun

Though this is supposed to be a grim day, the message of the stars is one of hope, especially for communications in your close relationship. It's rare you'll find yourself more in tune with your other half so try to keep the conversation flowing because this should sort out any recent problems.

Saturday, 14th October
Mercury direct

Another sign that relationship difficulties are being resolved is given by Mercury today. The tiny planet takes up a forward course and in so doing opens lines of communication that have been blocked. Misunderstandings can now be clearly and decisively sorted out.

Sunday, 15th October
Moon square Mercury

No sooner does Mercury open channels of communication than you're back into a cycle of misunderstanding and mistrust. Perhaps you aren't putting in sufficient effort to ensure clarity of speech. Take it slowly: wounds don't heal in ten minutes, so it's still important gently to renew the trust.

Monday, 16th October
Sun square Neptune

You may feel that recent difficulties are now behind you,

but you aren't quite out of the woods yet. The Sun's aspect to Neptune shows that self-deception is too easy. Be conscious of the care you have to take in both close relationships and in your career. Don't take anything at face value today.

Tuesday, 17th October
Moon trine Pluto

You've got some deep feelings and powerful frustrations bubbling inside you now, but you've got to exercise self-control. Try to be as logical as you can and don't let negative feelings like bitterness overwhelm your good sense. You could make unpleasant facts worse if you over-react now.

Wednesday, 18th October
Moon square Venus

There's an intimate feel to today's stars as the Moon and Venus are in aspect from romantic and sexual areas of your horoscope. This could herald a passionate embrace which, if not wise, is certainly enjoyable. In financial affairs, try not to spend too much on pleasure just now.

Thursday, 19th October
Mars conjunct Pluto

This should be the passionate highlight of the year. Mars and Pluto combine in the most intimate and sexual area of your chart encouraging sudden infatuations, sensual encounters and deep feelings. Face all your fears now and make them abandon their power over you. Questions of inheritance and investment also come to the fore today.

Friday, 20th October
Mars into Sagittarius

Your brainpower is enhanced as your ruler, Mars enters Sagittarius today. Your intellect, philosophical leanings and religious convictions are given a powerful boost now. Matters of education are also favourably influenced, as is anything associated with distant travel and foreign contacts.

Saturday, 21st October
Moon sextile Pluto

You can't get changes in the workplace out of your mind today. You may feel somewhat insecure if you get the slightest suggestion that your income is threatened. Don't over-react because your fears are groundless and changes at work will tend to favour your prospects.

Sunday, 22nd October
Moon conjunct Mercury

Spend today in the company of someone you love. You need some emotional reassurance and can only get it by an affectionate heart to heart. The beginnings of any sort of partnership, romantic or business is strongly favoured today.

Monday, 23rd October
Sun into Scorpio

Complex financial matters prove no challenge to you as the Sun moves into the sign of Scorpio from today. You should look at everything connected with inheritance and investment. A practical attitude is vital now since you've got the chance to set complex issues in order. This influence extends to the more intimate side of your existence too. Sexual affairs are highlighted and should assume their proper importance.

Tuesday, 24th October
Moon conjunct Sun

The New Moon emphasizes yesterday's message of shrewdness in investment. It's also time to look at any

sexual problems that have occurred and discuss them
without any embarrassment. You'll feel as if a weight has
lifted off your shoulders once you unburden your heart.

Wednesday, 25th October
Mercury sextile Jupiter, Venus trine Saturn

There's a complex set of planetary aspects today. Mercury
and Jupiter show that on the personal front there's an
expansiveness and joy bringing you into close harmony with
partners and friends. Venus' good aspect to Saturn shows
that in your inner life too, this harmony is reflected and
you'll feel at peace with yourself.

Thursday, 26th October
Moon conjunct Pluto

Self-love is equally as vital as loving someone else. That's
what you're learning now as the Moon conjuncts Pluto in
one of the most psychologically sensitive areas of your chart.
When you realize your own true worth, it's so much easier
to understand the value others place upon you.

Friday, 27th October
Moon square Saturn

Delays and frustrations abound on a day when the Moon
makes a stressful aspect to Saturn. Anything connected
with learning or travel is most prone to distraction and
petty annoyances. Keep calm Aries: today may be
challenging but you'll win through.

Saturday, 28th October
Venus sextile Neptune

Tread carefully today, because the feelings of those around
you are too sensitive to be tampered with. You need a lot
of tact just to get along now. In both work and family affairs
it's like walking on eggshells, yet you'd be well advised to

do just that if you want a peaceful life. At least you're in a sympathetic and understanding mood.

Sunday, 29th October
Moon sextile Venus

Though you have some faults, meanness isn't among them. You'll prove that statement today because you'll be determined not to stint on any luxury or enjoyment. A day out with the family could be expensive but it's also going to be fun.

Monday, 30th October
Moon sextile Pluto

You're taking more of a sober attitude to the financial realities of your life as the week begins. You know that there's some advantage to be had in making some long-term economic moves. Perhaps an investigation will reveal that there's a better way of using your cash to gain more interest, or a better investment to be made.

Tuesday, 31st October
Sun conjunct Mars

This should be a profitable day if you take advantage of the main chance to make money now. The practicalities of life dealt with, you'll be in the mood for some fun. When the Sun meets up with Mars in the most sexual area of your chart, that spells passion and intimate enjoyment.

November at a Glance

LOVE	♥	♥	♥	♥	♥
WORK	★	★			
MONEY	$	$	$	$	$
FITNESS	◓	◓			
LUCK	∪	∪	∪		

Wednesday, 1st November
Moon trine Mercury

November isn't the most attractive of months yet you could be in a holiday mood, ready to take a look outside your usual stamping grounds. Have some fun before winter really starts. Take your other half and set out to explore. You're about to meet new friends and look at life from a fresh perspective.

Thursday, 2nd November
Moon conjunct Saturn

The Aries independence has got a down side too. It has never been more apparent than today, when all that pioneering energy merely leaves you feeling isolated and out in the cold. You feel as if no one truly understands what you're about. Perhaps they don't, but give them time and they'll eventually catch up with your ideas.

Friday, 3rd November
Venus into Sagittarius

Venus enters the outgoing, exciting sign of Sagittarius giving you the impetus to prove some points and extend the borders of your knowledge. Your boldness and decisive attitudes will win respect now. A woman may show you that there are so many more areas to explore beyond anything you've previously known.

Saturday, 4th November
Mercury into Scorpio

Now your mental horizons are broadening, Mercury's entry into Scorpio gives you another chance to examine minutely the underlying reasons behind everything from financial commitments to personal mysteries that have irritated you. Curiosity is boundless as you probe beneath the surface of seemingly intractable problems. If solutions are to be found . . . you'll find them.

Sunday, 5th November
Moon square Uranus

Give an Aries a challenge and he or she will rise to the bait every time. That's the case today when you'll aggressively compete and seek to outdo anyone and anything. Of course it's sometimes a good idea to sit back and await developments, but that's not your style. The best of luck to you; you're going to need it.

Monday, 6th November
Moon opposite Mercury

You are far too emotional to make any sort of truly sensible decision today. You've got some intimate affair constantly at the back of your mind so when it comes to finances and the best use of cash leave it to another day when you can weigh up the pros and cons more effectively.

Tuesday, 7th November
Moon opposite Sun

The Full Moon has got the effect of bringing hidden matters to light now. Secrets, even embarrassing secrets come into the open in a surprising way. Your sexual relationships are at the centre of this process so you have the chance to put such matters on a more reasonable footing. Finances too need some attention now.

Wednesday, 8th November
Moon opposite Pluto

We're still on the vexed topic of money. This is not to suggest that you're totally materialistic, it's just that this area of your life really does need some attention now. Perhaps you're feeling insecure about your future so you need to make sure that your savings and investments are in order.

Thursday, 9th November
Moon opposite Venus

You know that you're a deeply sensitive person under all that bluster. It's a fact you don't much like sharing but the sympathetic and charitable side is apparent for all to see today. Leave business for another day and use this sentimental influence to express affection to someone you love.

Friday, 10th November
Moon square Saturn

It's hard to get your point across today. The question is, do you actually know what you want to say in the first place? The Moon's harsh aspect to Saturn is confusing at best so it's important you get your facts straight before you make any controversial statements.

Saturday, 11th November
Jupiter square Saturn

The harsh realities of life intrude too far for comfort now, as you realize that many of your hopes were simply pipe dreams. That's not to say that progress is impossible in these areas, it's just not going to be quite as easy as you thought. There are still plenty of opportunities for you so don't allow one setback to put you off totally.

Sunday, 12th November
Moon trine Mercury

Knowing who your friends are is very important to you at the moment, and it looks like you've got more supporters than even you thought you had, both inside and outside your family. It's therefore safe to come out into the open with your plans. You'll find an appreciative and keen audience.

Monday, 13th November
Moon opposite Uranus

Monday starts off on the wrong foot as far as you are concerned, and it'll take you some time to start again. The problem is that though you're bursting with originality, everyone else is too preoccupied by their own concerns to give you a fair hearing. It's time to paddle your own canoe. Others will catch up at their own pace.

Tuesday, 14th November
Moon square Mercury

Any agreements concerning such sensitive issues as inheritance, investments or even alimony will go nowhere if you give in to an emotional outburst today. Feelings are running high, so it's more important than ever that you keep a cool head. Don't let your heart intrude into matters of finance.

Wednesday, 15th November
Mars conjunct Jupiter

This is truly a marvellous day. Your ruling planet Mars joins with Jupiter to provide some stunning opportunities for your future progress. Don't be afraid to venture into the unknown because luck is more likely to be found there than in the old well-trodden pathways. Academic interests benefit from this vigorous mental attitude.

Thursday, 16th November
Sun sextile Neptune

You are willing to compromise sometimes, but when a work colleague suggests a scheme that doesn't go along with your personal ethics, you will not bend. This is the right course because your high-minded attitude will win through in business ventures while other, more shady deals will fail.

Friday, 17th November
Moon sextile Mercury

As the Moon contacts Mercury it's time to put your cards on the table. A meeting will work in your favour if you are open and honest in your opinions now. Don't be afraid to stand out from the crowd.

Saturday, 18th November
Venus square Saturn

Though news from a distance, whether personal or via the media seems nothing but bad, it isn't an excuse for you to lose your personal faith. 'It's better to light a candle than curse the dark', so apply that philosophy to your life now.

Sunday, 19th November
Venus conjunct Jupiter, Mercury sextile Neptune

This planetary influence is excellent both for you and your family. The two most fortunate planets Jupiter and Venus combine their forces to lift your spirits and add to your quota of love and happiness. Your fond dreams too are a step nearer to fulfilment as Mercury and Neptune encourage you to express your desires.

Monday, 20th November
Sun sextile Uranus

This is a day for brainwaves. The Sun makes positive contact with Uranus giving you a touch of genius in all professional and financial affairs. Your instincts are on course now simply because you can see past the obvious to what is possible. You're on the right road.

Tuesday, 21st November
Mercury sextile Uranus

You've got piercing insight today as the Uranian influence continues, making you impatient of distractions and focusing your attention on the nitty gritty. There's very little in business or intimate affairs that can get past your eagle eye today.

Wednesday, 22nd November
Sun into Sagittarius

The planetary message is expand your knowledge and experience as the Sun moves into Sagittarius. If you've been dissatisfied with your educational accomplishments then this is the time to think about improving your qualifications. Anything that takes your attention away from your usual round of activities is favoured now. Travel too should be very enjoyable for the next month.

Thursday, 23rd November
Venus conjunct Mars

Today's conjunction of Venus and Mars opens your eyes to numerous possibilities both in the romantic sense and on a more cultural level. The aspect is undoubtedly good for all affairs of the heart especially if you can share your insights with someone special. Art, music and theatre may also capture your interest.

Friday, 24th November
Moon conjunct Venus

Affairs of the heart are still the centre of your life as the Moon now meets Venus, lifting you to a new emotional peak. It's a sensitive influence which makes you aware of tender affection as opposed to fiery passion. It's still good to make plans for a journey.

Saturday, 25th November
Moon sextile Saturn

It's not often that you worry over every detail obsessively. Today's the exception because the Moon and Saturn make sure that your feet are on the ground and you don't miss a trick. Take your time now because it's better to double check your professional stance rather than be sorry later.

Sunday, 26th November
Moon conjunct Uranus

The conventional ways of getting things done hold little appeal today. Uranus again encourages you to look for alternatives in every sphere of life. Don't worry if you are thought of as being eccentric, there is method in your madness.

Monday, 27th November
Venus into Capricorn

It's obvious that to get on in the world you need more than aggressive drive to make your mark. Venus's entry into the career area adds a need for charm and diplomacy too. Women, especially those in authority will have a great influence for the next few weeks. You too will need to make a good impression.

Tuesday, 28th November
Moon sextile Mars

It's a time for you to show off your social skills. Friends, old and new are out there waiting for you. I'll bet you didn't know you were so popular. Go to any gathering and you'll be the centre of attention.

Wednesday, 29th November
Moon square Mercury

You may be getting a little too big for your boots at the moment. Though you claim all you do is in everyone's best interests, aren't you being a little self-serving about it? Be totally honest about your motives, at least to yourself and judge then.

Thursday, 30th November
Mars into Capricorn

Having used some Venusian soft soap in professional life, it's now time for drive, force and ambition. Yes, your ruling planet Mars has now entered the career area encouraging you to forge ahead with plans. You may feel you want to take a more independent course so this influence favours those who run their own businesses. You'll be very brash and forthright.

December at a Glance

LOVE	♥				
WORK	★	★	★	★	★
MONEY	$	$			
FITNESS	◕	◕	◕		
LUCK	U	U	U	U	U

Friday, 1st December
Moon square Mars

All this ambitious activity is bound to take its toll, and the Moon's aspect to Mars shows that you're probably exhausted by now. That generally means that you're irritable, so do yourself and everyone else a favour and take it easy for once.

Saturday, 2nd December
Moon trine Mercury

You're feeling more rational and in control today. You've got a pretty good idea of where you are going, and perhaps feel that you could do with a little help along the way. Adult education courses are available in nearly every field, so why not investigate the possibilities of broadening your knowledge now.

Sunday, 3rd December
Moon square Neptune

The vague or downright silly attitudes of someone around you may be irritating, but you should tolerate differences with calmness today. It may be that you're sick of the materialism of this season and need something a little more spiritual. But each to his own as they say. All the same don't believe everything you're told.

Monday, 4th December
Moon trine Venus

Anything connected with your work, ambitions and financial fortunes should go very well indeed today. This is a happy, positive day so you'll be quite content with your lot at the moment. Perhaps you're developing a value system that really gives you inner satisfaction.

Tuesday, 5th December
Mercury square Saturn

The truth is out today. If there have been any areas of your life that have looked a little shady, all will now be revealed. You may not like what you see, yet you know where you are and that's always easier to cope with. Now you'll know what to do next.

Wednesday, 6th December
Moon square Saturn

I don't know if it's in reaction to yesterday's revelations but there's a depressive influence around you at the moment. If you took some time to consider you'd see that you're in an advantageous position so minor hiccups shouldn't affect you so much.

Thursday, 7th December
Moon opposite Sun, Jupiter

The Full Moon crystallizes your ideas today. Those thoughts which have been vague and possibly disconcerting now come into focus and you'll find that your path is clear. Mind you, you are in the grip of a spendthrift impulse as well, but that's hard to avoid at this time of year.

Friday, 8th December
Mercury conjunct Jupiter

All this clarity of mind has given you renewed confidence, boosting your optimism no end. This is a good time to send off Christmas cards to friends in distant parts of the world. Show that those far away are still in your thoughts.

Saturday, 9th December
Moon opposite Venus .

Today should be an active one around the home; the trouble is that you'd far rather be left to your own devices at the moment. Everywhere you turn you find another demand from a family member who won't be easily put off. Visitors too prove to be a distraction. You'll have to grin and bear it this once.

Sunday, 10th December
Moon opposite Uranus

Traditional values leave you cold this Sunday as plans for the Christmas holiday are discussed. You'd far rather do something more adventurous than sit around doing the same old things you do every year. I think you might lose the argument on this one.

Monday, 11th December
Sun square Saturn

I don't know what's caused it but a lot of your fears resurface today, making you wonder whether you are doing the right thing at all. Remember that some parts of your life are secure no matter how much you worry about others. Try to wait a while; everything will fall into place.

Tuesday, 12th December
Mercury into Capricorn

Your position and status in life occupy central place as Mercury enters your fellow cardinal sign of Capricorn. If you're in any doubt that you've received the honours and rewards due to you then you've got a few weeks to set the record straight and get what's rightfully yours.

Wednesday, 13th December
Moon trine Mercury

Don't be afraid to seek out your boss or other authority figure with a well-thought out suggestion today. Employ a little tact and your point will be well made, doing your professional standing no end of good.

Thursday, 14th December
Moon trine Mars

You've got the urge to get your body in tip top condition before the festive season takes its yearly toll on your physique. This may not be the best time to start a diet but that isn't going to stop you now. Your health situation may be vaguely worrying: if that's so then seek out some professional advice to ease your mind.

Friday, 15th December
Moon trine Uranus

You're particularly rebellious and even eccentric today. Your ambitions are fiery and determined so no old-fashioned thinking is going to stand in your way. Today could signal a turning point in both your daily habits and career direction.

Saturday, 16th December
Moon square Mercury

A surprise or two tend to be good for any relationship since it keeps you on your toes. If you thought that you knew your other half inside out, then think again, because you'll be astonished by his or her actions and opinions now. It all serves to make life more interesting.

Sunday, 17th December
Venus conjunct Neptune

Though your ambitions are still occupying your thoughts, the conjunction of Venus and Neptune makes this a sensitive, often sentimental day. Music will have a profound effect on your mood. You need emotional reassurance now, but that's alright because the conjunction stimulates affection too.

Monday, 18th December
Moon sextile Mercury

If you can pick your way through the gossip and rumours in the workplace you can quite easily improve your position simply because you've got the ability to put two and two together. This is a progressive influence that'll aid your career security.

Tuesday, 19th December
Sun conjunct Jupiter

This is a day full of luck and happiness. The Sun meets up with Jupiter, boosting your confidence and vision. A person you meet could well open your eyes to the possibilities and opportunities that surround you. You'll feel a sense of rightness with the universe that's almost religious in nature. All in all, a very good day.

Wednesday, 20th December
Venus conjunct Uranus

This is the season for office parties so it doesn't stretch the imagination too far to suggest that the conjunction of Venus with Uranus means just that. There's an exciting atmosphere in which literally anything can happen. A few surprises are in store, and some of them are romantic in nature.

Thursday, 21st December
Venus into Aquarius

As if this time of year wasn't social enough, Venus enters your house of associations and friendships today casting a glamorous influence over all areas of fun and excitement. You won't be short of charm for a while and the energetic way in which you set out to enjoy yourself is staggering. The world is a happier place as far as you're concerned.

Friday, 22nd December
Moon conjunct Sun, Sun into Capricorn

The Sun enters Capricorn today marking the Winter Solstice, but before it adds to your initiative and career drive, it meets the Moon showing the great heights that you could possibly attain. The combined message is that there's nothing to fear except fear itself. Reach for the stars Aries, you've got it made.

Saturday, 23rd December
Mercury conjunct Mars

Even though Christmas is nearly upon us, your mind isn't fixed on the festivities just yet. In fact you're busy working out a career strategy that'll bring you the maximum of advantage with the minimum of fuss. You know it's going to be hard work, but you aren't afraid of that.

Sunday, 24th December
Moon conjunct Uranus

It's a good day to get out to visit friends old and new. Even if you didn't intend mixing socially, you'll find it's unavoidable since wherever you turn there's someone you know. A quick last-minute trip to the shops could turn into an all-day affair simply because of the number of people that run across your path.

Monday, 25th December
Mars sextile Saturn

If ever there was a time to forget old wounds and forgive, it's Christmas Day. The aspect between Mars and Saturn encourages a tolerant and charitable attitude now. Take this opportunity to make today a truly happy Christmas.

Tuesday, 26th December
Moon sextile Pluto

Some light-hearted argument is on the cards for today because you're prepared to stick up for what you believe in. In social situations a good debate on a topic of mutual interest will enliven the day and stimulate your mind.

Wednesday, 27th December
Moon sextile Mars

Though you tend to be a forthright person, you must realize that going at problems like a bull at a gate isn't always the answer. Some tact and subtlety is required if you're going to get your own way now. Pay attention to the finer feelings of those around you, and they'll again allow you to take the lead.

Thursday, 28th December
Mercury conjunct Neptune

It's not one of your logical days as Mercury meets Neptune and makes the world of dreams and fantasies more attractive than anything else. This, of course, is part of the creative process; we all need time to dream now and again. Steer clear of apparent bargains though, because you're far too susceptible to glib talkers now.

Friday, 29th December
Moon square Mars

In total contrast to yesterday's cloudy influences you're back to a go-getting, ambitious individual now. Second best isn't good enough for you and your quest for perfection is all consuming. You need to burn off all this energy constructively, so keep yourself occupied.

Saturday, 30th December
Moon square Neptune

It's obvious that you're on a see-saw of energy at the moment. You tend to be unaccountably tired today, and not quite with it as far as your duties are concerned. Take it easy, you've been through a lot recently and could do with a break.

Sunday, 31st December
Moon into Taurus

When you consider your life, it's not just the material things that matter, but the wealth of sentiment and regard in which you are held. The Taurean Moon highlights the positive views of others, and you'll feel a glow of contentment as this year draws to a close. It's good to have your priorities right isn't it.

Also by Sasha Fenton:

SUN SIGNS

Discover yourself and others through astrology

Much has been written about astrology and, in particular, Sun signs. However, in this unique book Sasha Fenton turns her inimitable astrological skills to the subject, revealing once and for all exactly what you want to know about your Sun sign.

Sign by sign, the book fully explains the significance of each sign, including such details as the Elements and the Qualities of each sign. It dispels any confusions regarding cusps or Summertime, and compares well-known celebrities with yourself. It will leave you with vital knowledge about health, hobbies, shopping habits, possessions, work, sex and, most important of all, not what it is like to *be* a particular sign, but what it is like to *live* with one.

MOON SIGNS

Discover the hidden power
of your emotions

Almost everyone knows their Sun sign and what it says about their basic personality. Rising signs reveal even more about their personality. But what does our Moon sign, the sign that governs our emotions, tell us?

The position of the Moon in our birthchart affects our deepest requirements, our innermost needs. It governs our attitudes to food, our unconscious motivations, our habits and, of course, our relationships. Complete with a simple, easy-to-use ephemeris to find your own Moon sign, Sasha Fenton's acclaimed book will help you to reveal the hidden power of your emotions – she even shows how your garden can benefit from an understanding of phases of the Moon.

RISING SIGNS

Discover the truth about
your personality

The sign of the zodiac rising on the eastern horizon when you are born – your Rising sign – reveals details about your outer personality and how it masks what is underneath: your looks, actions and outward behaviour may all be determined by your Rising sign. And, being based on the actual *time* of birth, it is a far more personal indicator of character than the more general Sun sign.

Here Sasha Fenton shows how to find your Rising sign and explains how it applies to you. In addition, she examines decanates, the modifying 'thirds' of the zodiac signs, and their subsidiary effects on the horoscope.

THE PLANETS

Discover the power
of the planets

The placing of the planets on a birthchart can have an extraordinary effect on the personality. This book gives a clear guide to the planets and to the way in which their energies work through the various signs and houses.

In a style which is simple for the beginner, yet packed with new and interesting information for the skilled astrologer, Sasha Fenton brings the planets alive by giving both brief and detailed descriptions of their properties. Fascinating facts about ruling, rising and retrograde planets, as well as more complex terminology, will provide a clear insight into the workings of each planet upon any birthchart.

UNDERSTANDING ASTROLOGY

First steps in chart interpretation

Understanding Astrology provides a concise introduction to the ancient art of astrology, showing how it can be used to assess a person's character. Ingenious short-cuts and quick-clue summaries are given to help the beginner quickly grasp the basic ideas, and all aspects of astrology are covered, from elements, houses and hemispheres to planets and their influence.

Complete with diagrams, sample birth charts and a glossary of terms, this book serves as an ideal starting point for anyone taking their first steps in the fascinating study of astrology.